T0330412

Household Debt and Economic Crises

Household Debt and Economic Crises

Causes, Consequences and Remedies

Heikki Hiilamo

Professor of Social Policy, University of Helsinki, Finland

 Edward Elgar
PUBLISHING

Typeset by Columns Design XML Ltd, Reading

Published by
Edward Elgar Publishing Limited
The Lypiatts
15 Lansdown Road
Cheltenham
Glos GL50 2JA
UK

Edward Elgar Publishing, Inc.
William Pratt House
9 Dewey Court
Northampton
Massachusetts 01060
USA

A catalogue record for this book
is available from the British Library

Library of Congress Control Number: 2018939991

This book is available electronically in the **Elgar**online
Social and Political Science subject collection
DOI 10.4337/9781785369872

ISBN 978 1 78536 986 5 (cased)
ISBN 978 1 78536 987 2 (eBook)

Typeset by Columns Design XML Ltd, Reading
Printed and bound in Great Britain by TJ International Ltd, Padstow

Contents

Figures and tables

FIGURES

TABLES

Preface

Feeling indebted is more obvious in the context of this book than in my previous works. While writing this book I have stepped on the shoulders of a large number of senior scholars and professionals during a period which extends to three decades. My personal interest in over-indebtedness goes back to my early working life. I worked as a journalist with a degree in economics and some university studies in law at the time when the Finnish economy was going through a period of overheating before a complete collapse in 1991. While reporting for a national newspaper, *Uusi Suomi*, my bosses, Olli Ainola, Eero Karisto and Jyrki Vesikansa, gave me unexpected responsibility for following the banking crisis, which included bank takeovers, direct monetary assistance and temporary blanket guarantees to the banks – the crisis cost roughly 8 per cent of gross national product (GNP), making it the most severe of the contemporary Nordic banking crises. The financial institutions were bailed out while thousands of individuals were left with insurmountable debt burdens. The public atmosphere was filled with anger and resentment. After a career in journalism, Professor Olli Kangas introduced me to social policy and poverty research, which became my main area of academic interest.

Although I soon realized that poverty research has mainly ignored the topic of over-indebtedness, the original idea for this book did not come before a project funded by the Academy of Finland (SA 259 216, 2012–2016) which focused on the social consequences of economic recessions. With Jenni Blomgren and Nico Maunula, my good colleagues at the Social Insurance Institution of Finland research department, I was able to purchase and utilize a unique register from Suomen Asiakastieto Oy, a company maintaining the leading database of consumer and business credit history in Finland. The records of previously over-indebted persons were erased retrospectively following the amendment to the Credit Information Act taking effect on 1 April 2010, which stipulated that all outdated payment default entries had to be removed from the credit information register after the payment liability had expired. We got the personal identification numbers of 37 000 persons with default payment records whose name had been on the register for at least

15 years. The project resulted in one of the first register-based studies on consequences of over-indebtedness in the Nordic area.

As part of the same project I produced, together with Elina Turunen, a systematic literature review on the health effects of over-indebtedness. In 2013, I moved to the University of Helsinki, where Chaitawat Boonjubun, Meng Han Chau, Annika Lehmus-Sun and Jonni Tanskanen worked as my research assistants. Jonni Tanskanen also wrote his Masters' thesis utilizing the data described above. Chaitawat Boonjubun and Meng Han Chau carried out literature reviews which I was able to use in compiling this book. Annika Lehmus-Sun helped me with editing the references.

I have been privileged to have comments and guidance on my manuscript from Aapo Hiilamo, Elli-Alina Hiilamo, Juha Panzar and Anu Rajas. Johanna Niemi gave valuable comments on legal terms. I also am grateful to VID Specialized University Oslo, which offered me an opportunity to work as Kjell Nordstokke guest professor during the most intensive writing period in this project in 2017. I want to thank my boss Annette Peter-Leis and my colleagues Hans Morten Haugen, Kari Jordheim and Kari Korslien for their encouragement and support.

There is also a more personal reason behind my engagement with over-indebtedness. In 1991 my parents' textile company filed for bankruptcy, leaving some 100 people without work and my parents with unbearable debts due to personal liability of business loans. I am deeply indebted to my father Simo and my mother Pirkko, who showed how it is possible to recover from serious over-indebtedness with determination and a resourceful mind. While they were able to rebound soon, the bankruptcy continues to shadow their lives and the lives of my brothers and sisters to the present day. Through this personal experience I have come to realize how deep and long-standing the effects of a period of insolvency can be on concerned individuals and their families.

1. Context of debt problems

On 14 July 1656 Dutch painter and art collector Rembrandt Harmensz van Rijn (1606–1669) made it known to the Court of Holland in Amsterdam that he could not pay his creditors due to losses suffered in business as well as damage and losses at sea. Since that day the bankruptcy of a celebrated artist has struck people as an incidence of fantastic irony. To avoid imprisonment Rembrandt applied for *cessio bonorum,* a process stipulated by the Romans whereby debtors voluntarily surrender goods to creditors. As a result of personal bankruptcy, the 50-year-old painter was forced to cede possession not only of his own works but also of a large collection of paintings and drawings by other Old Masters. In addition were ceded busts of Roman emperors, suits of Japanese armour (among many other objects from Asia) and items of natural history, including minerals. These items were offered for sale in 1657 and 1658 but the prices were disappointing. As a result, Rembrandt had to also sell his house and printing-press in Sint Anthonisbreestraat[1] and move to a small rented apartment on Rozengracht 184, where he lived in poverty until his death. The famous painter was buried in an unmarked grave, and after 20 years his remains were taken away and destroyed, as was customary with poor people at that time.

The 20th and 21st centuries have witnessed tremendous developments in terms of better health, higher incomes and stronger states to support people in need. In the Western world, epidemic diseases have been more or less conquered, and earlier causes of death have been replaced by modern and degenerative diseases linked to lifestyles, stress and excess consumption (Grand 2008). Instead of epidemics another type of disease is causing havoc by destroying people's health, taking away their incomes and possessions and undermining the state's capacity to help people in need. That epidemic is over-indebtedness.

It might sound odd to call a problem related to the economic sphere of life an epidemic. The justification is twofold. Firstly, as will be presented in this book, over-indebtedness causes serious harm to health and well-being. Secondly, over-indebtedness is also highly contagious. Of

---

[1] Later Jodenbreestraat, and now the location of the Rembrandt museum.

course, it does not happen through the spread of disease agents from one individual to another, but through societal structures. Therefore the connections between individual suffering and social structures will also be explored in this book.

Throughout the 1980s and 1990s a number of Western countries went through periods of economic recession resulting in unprecedented numbers of over-indebted households, that is, households no longer able to meet their financial commitments. Over-indebtedness has affected and continues to affect a substantial share of private households in all economically advanced countries. It has negative effects on debtors and their dependants in terms of health and well-being. Over-indebtedness also relates to outcomes in the labour markets, financial markets, public revenues, welfare states, health care systems and judicial systems (Heuer 2013). The debt epidemic achieved gigantic proportions during the Global economic crises. For example, in the US the Great Recession destroyed 8 million jobs between 2007 and 2009, and more than 4 million homes were foreclosed (Mian and Sufi 2015a, p. 2).

Before the onslaught of the Global economic crises in 2008, studies on the consequences of debt problems were few and far between. Only a few classic studies have dealt with debt (see Caplovitz 1963, 1974, 1979; Ford 1988 as exceptions). For example, the large body of literature on welfare state regimes or models completely ignores the regulation of consumer finance and personal insolvency (for example Esping-Andersen 1990). Even later, the study of over-indebtedness has been plagued by short-sightedness. The question of over-indebtedness has been approached from a number of quite separate and not well-connected perspectives. Economists have studied the effect of household debt on macro-economic performance. The personal traits of over-indebted individuals have been the topic of social-psychologists. Social-epidemiologists have attempted to analyse the complex relationship between health and over-indebtedness, whereas scholars of law have, among other topics, compared different insolvency regimes from a juridical perspective.

The key notion of this book is that the combination of these perspectives is necessary in order to gain a more thorough understanding of over-indebtedness. This book aims to do that through a social policy paradigm where over-indebtedness is understood as a social risk, that is, a factor endangering or preventing the full participation of individuals in society. This paradigm aims also to find remedies to prevent and alleviate the over-indebtedness epidemic. The basic assumption in this inquiry is that collective action – that is, social policies – is needed to tackle the over-indebtedness epidemic.

We will analyse households and families who default on their debts, while covering all debt types that are used for individual purposes, from credit cards to mortgages. Most of the current research focuses on consumer debts. However, as the case of Rembrandt illustrates, the distinction between consumer debts and business-related debts is sometimes difficult to draw. Entrepreneurs and self-employed persons may have assumed individual responsibility to guarantee funding or individuals given surety for family members' or friends' business loans. Consequently, we also discuss business debts to the extent they result in individual liability.

This book acknowledges that debt and its consequences are bound to existing social structures. This is illustrated, for example, by the fact that debt problems have a gendered dimension (Goode 2009). Women are at higher risk of financial strain than men due to women's weaker position in the labour market. Women have lower wages and higher poverty rates. They are also more often single heads of households with children, and tend to lose out economically in the event of divorce. As a result, we may assume that financial strain and debt burden could affect women more strongly. On the other hand, when men have sole responsibility for managing incomes constrained by over-indebtedness, they reportedly experience anxiety and depression more typically than women (Goode 2012a). However, male pride in relation to financial matters may act as a barrier to seeking advice. This effect is aggravated by the fact that male pride in relation to financial matters forms a significant component of men's identities.

This book takes a general view on over-indebtedness and reflects the role of gender only in passing. We also acknowledge that causes, consequences and correlates of over-indebtedness are also affected by other socio-economic variables such as household structure, age, education, migrant status and disability (Patel et al. 2012). Nevertheless, these dimensions will be largely ignored for the sake of clarity and brevity while, we argue, more in-depth research is needed to understand the intersectional and multidimensional nature of debt problems.

As an academic discipline, social policy analyses both the nature of the risk and its consequences in a given social context, and discusses public policies to deal with the social risk. In this paradigm identifying the risk and its special features comes before analysing policies to handle the risk. That is also the path followed in this book. The main argument of over-indebtedness as a unique social risk is presented by: first, discussing the definition of over-indebtedness; then by focusing on causes and consequences of over-indebtedness; and, finally, by analysing the policies to prevent and/or alleviate over-indebtedness. Since no survey or register study was conducted for the single purpose of this book, the contribution of this inquiry lies mostly in the conceptual and theoretical arena. The aim is to demonstrate that over-indebtedness should be tackled with a more comprehensive and integrated set of public policies than in place today.

STRUCTURE OF THE BOOK

Before looking into the context of debt problems in six countries analysed in this book, we will briefly discuss a larger context of over-indebtedness among the rich countries, together with substantial issues relating to concepts and theoretical approaches. In the following section, we discuss debt collection and debt discharge; that is, the procedures relating to establishing payment default and consequent actions in six countries. We then analyse what causes people to become default-debtors. After that we focus on the consequences of over-indebtedness. Finally, we analyse public policies to prevent and/or alleviate over-indebtedness.

DEBT, REPAYMENT NORMS AND RELIGION

The essence of over-indebtedness is a breach of contract. A debt is left unpaid. This is foremost a moral problem on a individual level but one with a wide range of societal dimensions. The Latin phrase *Pacta sund servanda* is the foundation of any organized society, meaning that *agreements have to be binding*. Money and credit are inherently relational constructions operating through (tacit or explicit) contracts between people. The term "credit" (credibility → credo) reflects the moral and the legal background of the initial concept of lending money and entering into a relationship between creditor and borrower (debtor). Trust and personal responsibility are key elements in the morality of "credit".

The legislative history of the European consumer "bankruptcy" laws is rich with references to the sanctity of contracts (Heuer 2013). The repayment norm is even present in major religions, which is reflected in the fact that there is a surprising similarity between the language of religion and the language of finance (debt). That is the case in all Indo-European languages, where debt is repeatedly associated with guilt and sin, while payment is associated with salvation. Take, for example, the English words "guilt" and "redemption". In the German language, the words for guilt (*Schuld*) and debt (*Schulden*) carry almost similar meaning. The Lord's Prayer ("Our Father"), which has a central role in Christian worship, has even been translated to include a verse: "And forgive us our debts, as we forgive our debtors." Evidently, already during the time the Bible was written debt was a major problem underlying political and everyday life.

Given the moral norm behind the relationship between debtor and borrower, it is not surprising that religion still plays a role in over-indebtedness. Kiesel and Noth (2016) argue that while debt is discussed critically in Protestant history and writings, contrary to Catholicism, it also involves elements of a positive attitude towards debt. They find that the more widespread Catholicism is, the lower the share of over-indebted persons. In Islamic contexts, using microdata for Pakistan, Baele et al. (2014) find loans less likely to be defaulted on during Ramadan and in cities where religious-political parties receive a high share of votes.

The significance of repayment norm has been recognized since ancient times, and violation of the norm has been regulated with violent force. By default, incapable debtors are considered as "undeserving poor" (Townsend 1979). The "deserving poor" are those who are poor through no fault of their own – for example through illness, accident or age, or because of a lack of work – while the undeserving poor are poor because of laziness or personal problems including excessive debts. However, the repayment norm also reflects the power imbalance between creditors and debtors. Indeed, the Bible states that: "The rich rules over the poor, and the borrower is the slave of the lender" (Proverbs 22:7). According to the Norwegian scholar Christian Poppe (2008, p. 17), "this rule has been enforced through history with the full range of penalties for failing to repay debts, including various forms of physical punishment, enslave-ment and even death penalty". For example, in medieval Britain, dis-honest default-debtors faced the risk of being placed in the pillory, having their ears cut off, or even being killed. In the English language, the same word, "delinquent", is used for a person who commits a felony and a person who fails to repay a debt.

Moreover, the current social order is built on repayment norm, which is of paramount importance for financial markets (Poppe 2008). If a debt is unpaid not only is a fundamental convention in society challenged but also the very existence of money economy is put in jeopardy. Evidently, the value of any currency would collapse if a large enough number of debtors announced that they were not repaying their loans. Even today those people who are deemed as neglecting their financial commitments are still subject to a variety of debt collection procedures ranging from foreclosure to imprisonment. The causes and consequences of these present-day procedures are discussed in this book.

A fundamental feature of a credit contract is indeed the fact that it is not an agreement between equally powerful parties. In essence, the contract is between a party with extra resources and a party lacking resources. To put it simply, society is divided into two distinct, largely non-overlapping categories: the haves and the have nots – that is, those who have money to lend and those who need to borrow money (see Mian and Sufi 2015a). The composition of these categories gives a measure of wealth inequality in a society.

Neglecting a due payment is obviously a breach of the social norm which dictates that agreements are binding. The studies of present-day European debtors suggest that they feel quite guilty about their inability to fulfil their obligations (Kilborn 2005). Evidently, the government is required to intervene to enforce social order and to strike a balance between the rights of the debtor and the creditor. At this point the government and society as a whole tend to side with the stronger party, the creditor. Without denying society's concerns about enforcing social commitments, this book sides with the weaker party, the debtor. We focus on individual and household level over-indebtedness from the debtor's perspective, with emphasis on social policy measures, where over-indebtedness is considered a (new) social risk – a condition which should be regulated through public policies.

WHY HAS DEBT BECOME A PROBLEM IN DEVELOPED COUNTRIES?

Credit relates to three distributive systems of modern society: namely, markets, governmental actions and informal personal networks (Polanyi 1944). Credit is an important tool for economic progress and social welfare. Credit is involved in all household financial transactions, from shopping at a grocery store to acquiring property. Through new consumer credit products and aggressive marketing practices we have witnessed a financialization and commercialization of human interactions as more and more social interactions have been transferred into the realm of the market, using credit as a central valuation metric. It is obvious that normal wage-earning households need to take out credit to afford expensive purchases such as cars or houses. Debt is increasingly used also as a tool for financing smaller consumer needs.

The developed societies encourage their citizens to make debts in order to promote economic growth. Debt is used for private consumption. It is the lubricant which keeps the economy's wheels running. Democratization of credit means that property, goods and services are distributed among the population. Credit concerns also governmental redistributive systems of taxes, benefits, fees and fines. Credit and debt may also arise from transactions between private individuals, such as borrowing money from relatives or friends. Personal networks are also involved when loans are taken from the black market or when they relate to illegal activities, for example drug trafficking.

Credit gives access, even for those with small incomes, to a wide range of socially important items – ranging from life necessities to luxuries (Poppe 2008, p. 33). However, that is only possible as long as the debtors are able and willing to repay their loans. If a debtor is turned into a default-debtor, the process is reversed and credit will become excluding. A series of sanctions come into play, increasingly punitive up to the point where the debtors are not only blocked from further access to credit but also where they are even no longer able to guarantee basic necessities for life. They will no longer be able to engage in ordinary social activities, which will then quickly narrow and threaten to jeopardize their social identity (Poppe 2008).

So why have household debts become a problem (in developed countries) over the last few decades? The simple explanation is that credit has become ubiquitous, also described as the "democratization of credit availability". The use of credit cards has increased dramatically since the 1960s. In the mid-1960s they were largely unknown. By the second decade in the new millennium approximately 70 per cent of households participate in the credit card market in the US; 45 per cent in the mortgage market; 19 per cent in student loans; and 30 per cent in car loans (also 50 per cent hold stocks directly or indirectly) (Zinman 2015). These figures are from a cross-section of society; virtually almost everyone participates in the credit market during their life course.

However, it is worth noting that credit is not only a modern way to finance consumption. Before the dawn of the credit card industry, pawnbroking served working-class communities and helped them manage poverty (although the temperance movement preached against the pawnbroker's role in financing drinking). According to one estimate, there were nearly 1000 registered and some 50 000 unregistered money-lenders in England and in Wales in 1925. Butchers, drapers, plumbers and other traders allowed their customers to pay weeks, months and sometimes years after the goods or services were delivered (Ford 1988, pp. 15–16). Hire purchase of sewing machines, pianos, furniture and later cars, and mail order companies preceded the breakthrough of credit cards. Attitudes towards the use of credit were different, though. In the

18th and 19th centuries the wealthy and the emerging middle class expressed a dislike of credit used by poorer members of society. This attitude is visible, for example, through many proverbs, such as: "Better to go to bed supperless than rise in credit"; "He that borrows must pay again with shame and loss"; "Out of debt, out of danger"; and "Neither a borrower nor a lender be" (Ford 1988, p. 29).

During the "roaring twenties" in the US technological innovation brought new consumer products such as automobiles and radios into consumer markets (Igan et al. 2012). Financial innovations such as instalment plans made it easier for households to obtain credit to buy these coveted new items. General Motors (GM) was the first car maker to offer loans for the purchase of its automobiles. In 1991, GM established the General Motors Acceptance Corporation, and by 1927 two-thirds of new cars were purchased on instalment. Ford and Rootes followed GM's example, as did manufacturers of electronic goods such as Pye, Electrolux and, more recently, Hitachi.

Norwegian researcher Christian Poppe (2008, p. 12) argues that most Western capitalist societies underwent a change during the 1970s and 1980s: from "save first, pay cash" to "buy now, pay later". Credit became a device to include also those of limited means in mainstream consumer society. For the financial industry credit was no longer used as a means to finance consumption; rather, the sale of credit became an end in itself. Taking out credit was no longer connected to any negative morality. On the contrary, credit carried a promised individual advancement. Today credit is the necessary medium for a better life for all individuals with no inherited wealth.

THE CONTEXT OF DEBT PROBLEMS IN SIX COUNTRIES

The causes and consequences of debt problems, as well as policies to alleviate them, are context bound. This book adopts a comparative approach to the topic. We focus on two Anglo-Saxon countries (the US and the UK), together with two continental European countries (Germany and the Netherlands) and two Nordic countries (Finland and Norway). These six countries cover three different welfare state regimes, namely liberal, conservative and socio-democratic (Esping-Andersen 1990). These countries, as will be later demonstrated, will also fall into different categories in terms of debt collection and personal insolvency regimes and credit-based social policy orientations. While some countries get more coverage than others (for example due to specific causes of household indebtedness or availability of data and research evidence), across different chapters there will be (some) discussion on all six countries.

With its leading role among the capitalist countries the US is an obvious choice for analysis. The new innovations in consumer finance, most notably the use of credit cards, have been developed in the US and across the world from there. The US has weakly developed welfare state structures which are counterbalanced by consumer-friendly bankruptcy legislation to deal with cases of over-indebtedness. Moreover, the US credit and bankruptcy systems serve as internal models to be either emulated or avoided by other countries (Ramsay 2017, p. 7). The same holds true for the UK, or more specifically England and Wales (for more discussion see the following chapter). A number of path-breaking studies on consumer over-indebtedness have been conducted in these two countries (Caplovitz 1963, 1974, 1979; Ford 1988).

Credit has become a more central component of the German welfare state, with gradual erosion of savings promotions, the expansion of quasi-public loan schemes and the restructuring of the welfare state since the mid-1970s (Mertens 2017). Germany has a fledgling consumer insolvency legislation which emphasizes the role of debt counselling. Authorized debt counsellors have a mandated role in the German credit default legislation, and the country regularly publishes very comprehensive statistics on over-indebtedness.

With regard to over-indebtedness, the Netherlands is an interesting case among the continental European welfare states. The Dutch are the most indebted households in the euro area, in part because of tax benefits for leverage and high housing prices (OECD 2017a). At the end of 2015, almost one-third of Dutch homeowners had negative equity. As opposed to the US and the UK, the Dutch legal system provides limited options for debt restructuring. Mortgage debtors who have negative equity will not rely on the consumer insolvency procedure, which might not result in debt discharge. This regime, described as "draconian", encourages Dutch households to curb consumption and prioritize debt repayment (Klein 2016).

The decision to choose two Nordic countries relates to partly converging and partly diverging economic development and the similar scope of debt problems. The Northern European welfare states with populations ranging from 5 million (Denmark, Norway and Finland) to 10 million (Sweden) were hit by a severe economic recession in the late 1980s and early 1990s (Kiander and Vartia 2011). This was a direct result of deregulation of the economy in general and deregulation of financial markets in particular (Poppe et al. 2016). First in Norway, then Finland many people who had to sell their housing due to unemployment and/or skyrocketing mortgage interests were left with large debts when housing prices went down. For example, in Finland from 1990 to 1997 the number of people with payment default entry in the credit information register increased from 200 000 to more than 350 000 (Blomgren et al. 2016). Again, the economic collapse of 2008 led to an unprecedented period of stagnation in Finland, while similar development was not observed in Norway. In July 2017 the number of people with a payment default entry in Finland was a record almost 373 000 (Suomen Asiakastieto 2017), while there were 449 512 debtors in enforcement (Findikaattori 2017).

The Organisation for Economic Co-operation and Development's statistics on household debt (OECD 2017a, 2017b) show diverging paths of household indebtedness among the six countries (Figure 1.1).[2] The Netherlands clearly had the highest level of household debt from 1995 to 2015 as a percentage of national domestic income (NDI). In fact, the Netherlands is completely in its own league: except for 2001, its debt level increased continuously from 1995 to 2010, after which it decreased until 2016, reaching the same level as in 2007. Norway had the second highest debt level, which increased practically through the period. The UK and the US show a similar trajectory, with increase until the Global economic crisis and slow decrease in indebtedness thereafter. Germany diverges from the other countries. Household debt there increased from 1995 only to 2001, after which indebtedness began to fall continuously towards 2016. Finland shows a complete opposite trajectory, with slightly decreasing indebtedness before 2001 and continuous increase since then.

These figures also demonstrate that the effects of the Global economic crises were far from over in 2016. As a response to the crises central banks have adopted comprehensive policies to increase liquidity in the

---

[2] The OECD defines household debt as "all liabilities that require payment or payments of interest or principal by household to the creditor at a date or dates in the future". Consequently, all debt instruments are liabilities, but some liabilities – such as shares, equity and financial derivatives – are not considered as debt. According to the 1993 System of National Accounts (SNA), debt is thus obtained as the sum of the following liability categories, whenever available in the financial balance sheet of the households and non-profit institutions serving the household sector, such as: currency and deposits; securities other than shares, except financial derivatives; loans; insurance technical reserves; and other accounts payable. For households, liabilities predominantly consist of loans, in particular mortgage loans for the purchase of houses. This indicator is measured as a percentage of NDI (for data see SNA 2008).

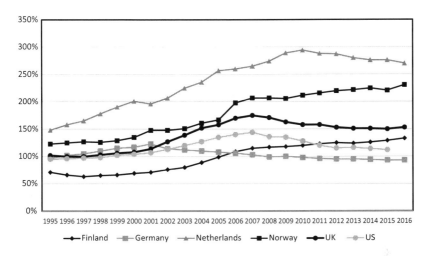

Source: OECD (2017a, 2017b).

Figure 1.1   Household debt as share of national domestic income in six countries between 1995 and 2015/2016

financial markets by zero level interest rates and bond purchase programmes. The record low interest rates have increased house prices and encouraged consumers to take out big loans to finance, for example, housing purchases. That is the case especially in Finland and Norway, where household indebtedness reached record levels in 2016. The near zero level interest rates have also fuelled housing investment speculation (Poppe et al. 2016). This time the development does not concern single countries but all countries where central banks have flooded the economies with cheap money. As the old cautious wisdom goes, it is not possible to spot a bubble before it bursts. If this happens, the Western countries may experience over-indebtedness to extents never experienced before.

The OECD figures for 2014–2016 shown in Table 1.1 indicate that the great majority of households had outstanding liabilities in all countries except Germany (OECD 2017b). This notion of "indebted households" excludes households having a balance on their credit card (or utility bills) on which no interest payment is paid, but includes those households that have payment arrears on their credit cards. These figures can hardly be taken as a measure of over-indebtedness; rather, they reflect payment cultures and the use of credit in different countries. A more serious measure of risk of over-indebtedness is a debt-to-asset ratio above 75 per cent of income. The United States and Norway had the highest share of households in this category (30 per cent and 21 per cent respectively), followed by the Netherlands. The column "households with debt-to-income ratio above three" in Table 1.1 indicates that the Netherlands and Norway had the highest numbers by this measure. Different measures produce slightly different country rankings, but they show that Norway, the Netherlands and the US are the countries with the highest risk of household over-indebtedness. The figures and rankings for the countries by the three measures were almost similar in 2010–2012.

Table 1.1   Share of indebted households by three different measures in six OECD countries

Country	Year	Indebted households (outstanding liabilities)	Rank	Debt-to-asset ratio above 75%	Rank	Households with debt-to-income ratio above three	Rank
Finland	2014	57.4%	5	13.6%	4	5.5%	5
Germany	2014	45.1%	6	11.0%	5	4.0%	6
Netherlands	2015	65.7%	3	17.9%	3	32.2%	1
Norway	2014	84.9%	1	29.5%	1	28.2%	2
United Kingdom	2015	61.0%	4	4.5%	6	9.6%	4
United States	2016	77.2%	2	20.9%	2	13.0%	3

Source: OECD (2017b).

It is important to note that the three types of debt that are commonly attributed to social policy area – housing (mortgages), educational (student loans) and medical (credit card) – are also associated with over-indebtedness. Therefore, access to consumer credit debt settlement or consumer bankruptcy is also an important element of credit-based social policy. Interestingly, the Anglo-liberal welfare state model has a compensatory character as opposed to continental European and Nordic welfare state models where defaulters are offered easy access to a process that guarantees a fresh new start for default-debtors. The more a credit-based social policy is promoted, the higher the risks households have to bear. These risks are socio-economically unequally distributed.

The unequal distribution can, however, be amended through a market-based insolvency regime. Angel and Heitzmann (2015) show that households in countries with no or only weak discharge possibilities are more likely to be over-indebted as their chances of exiting over-indebtedness are smaller.

WHAT IS OVER-INDEBTEDNESS?

A debt, whether small or large, is not a sign of financial problems as such. Indeed it may even indicate a high level of solvency. Actually, highly indebted households tend to have relatively high incomes and wealth. Therefore, a high level of borrowing is not necessarily an indication of inability to meet commitments. Among the wealthy, having large debts has never gone out of fashion; leveraging has been the way to riches for many present-day tycoons. A debt only becomes a problem when the debtor is unable to repay it on time.

Over-indebtedness is not a continuous variable, but rather a dichotomous variable. This notion pays attention to the particular change when individuals turn from indebted into over-indebted. Poverty is also a dichotomous or a category variable (Townsend 1979). However, a change of status from non-poor to poor, be it by absolute or relative definition of poverty, is different from a change of status from indebted to over-indebted. Objective poverty status is always tied to a certain level of resources or consumption, whether expressed in absolute or relative terms. The difference between poverty and over-indebtedness boils down to the fact that poverty is measured by income, which is a continuous variable, while over-indebtedness is exclusively a category variable.

Further clarification of the distinction between poverty and over-indebtedness is obtained by distinguishing between two types of household (Poppe 2008, p. 34; Poppe et al. 2016). The first is the "cash-flow household", which needs all available income to cover necessary daily expenses. As a consequence, this household type is largely unable to save and invest, and instead is left to consume most of the credit it takes on. In cases where the equalized incomes of this household fall below a certain amount, it is considered as suffering poverty. The second type is the "investment household", which may have income just above the bare minimum, allowing its members to take advantage of other kinds of capital than their own labour by saving money and using credit as a means to build assets such as property and education. If an "investment household" gets into financial difficulties with debts and is forced to adopt the financial career of a poor "cash-flow household", describing the household's situation through poverty would ignore the important change, typical for example among mortgage defaulters, from "investment household" to "cash-flow household".

Finally, we need to make one more distinction between poverty and over-indebtedness. The experience of poverty is related to the larger social context of where individuals and families live; and the conditions of poor individuals and households are mediated through a complex network of actors such as welfare agencies, employers and family members. That is also true for over-indebtedness; but there is also a special relationship between the debtor and the creditor, which is the single most important determinant for the experience of over-indebtedness.

It is not difficult to provide simple descriptions of over-indebtedness. Firstly, generally speaking over-indebtedness can be defined as a situation in which a debtor is permanently unable to repay a debt. Secondly, a more sophisticated definition takes into account the resources available for servicing a debt. By this definition an individual or household (assuming that resources are pooled within a household) is over-indebted if the debt cannot be sustained in relation to current earnings and any additional resources raised from the sale (under fair conditions) of real or financial assets. Thirdly, it is necessary to consider the effects of over-indebtedness. There is a theoretical case where a person has deliberately chosen to live his or her life with unpaid financial commitments, and is not harmed by that choice. Over-indebtedness becomes a problem when it is accompanied by suffering and trauma for those affected.

The critical element in defining over-indebtedness concerns the inability to pay. How then to define the instance when a person or a household is not able to pay debts? When does the situation become unbearable enough to be taken as an "inability to pay"? It is challenging to come up with an exact definition of a situation which would be both measurable and comparable across time and place. Despite decades of scholarly and administrative work there is no consensus in the literature on how to define over-indebtedness (CPEC 2013; D'Alessio and Iezzi 2013). According to D'Alessio and Iezzi, empirical studies of over-indebtedness have instead tended to converge on a common set of indicators reflecting four aspects of over-indebtedness: making high repayments relative to income; being in arrears; making heavy use of credit; and finding debt a burden (Table 1.2). Using data from the Bank of Italy's survey on Italian households the authors showed that different measures of over-indebtedness end up identifying different households with debts. About 8 per cent of households were over-indebted according to at least one indicator, but no more than 2 per cent were over-indebted according to two indicators simultaneously. The condition of over-indebtedness according to these indicators rarely coincided with the subjective condition of economic distress. The subjective measures of over-indebtedness may raise concerns of comparability. There is no reason to reject these measures, though. Subjective measures of debt burden may have an important role to play in understanding debt and its psycho-social consequences. The subjective perception of debt burden carries the direct impact of debts on individuals. Objective indicators may not give a complete picture of the pressures of debt as there are often unobserved factors that may make debt a problem (Keese 2012).

Table 1.2 Common indicators of over-indebtedness

Category	Indicator
Cost of servicing debt	Households spending more than 30% (or 50%) of their gross monthly income on total borrowing repayments (secured and unsecured)
	Households spending more than 25% of their gross monthly income on unsecured repayments
	Households whose spending on total borrowing repayments takes them below the poverty line
Arrears	Households more than 2 months in arrears on a credit commitment or household bill
Number of loans	Households with 4 or more credit commitments
Subjective perception of debt burden	Households declaring that their borrowing repayments are a "heavy burden"

Source: D'Alessio and Iezzi (2013).

After discussing the pros and cons of the measures suggested in Table 1.2, D'Alessio and Iezzi conclude that they all are, for the most part, measures of the process of becoming over-indebted, rather than measures of the outcome associated with having problems with debts (see also Haas 2006). Recognizing the ambiguities in previous definitions of over-indebtedness, a comprehensive EU study on over-indebtedness proposed a broader definition (CPEC 2013, pp. 19–31). By this definition, "over-indebted households include those who face difficulties meeting (or falling behind with) their commitments, whether these relate to servicing secured or unsecured borrowing or to payment of rent, utility or other household bills on ongoing basis". With this definition over-indebtedness may be measured, for example, through credit arrears, credit defaults, utility/rent arrears or the use of administrative procedures such as consumer insolvency proceedings.

ADMINISTRATIVE DEFINITION OF OVER-INDEBTEDNESS

Over-indebtedness can be also approached from a legal perspective. All developed societies have official legal mechanisms or institutions to collect money or property equivalent to the overdue debt (Niemi-Kiesiläinen 1999). The most obvious legal definition of debt problems or over-indebtedness is precisely the moment when a debtor is turned into a default-debtor in the eyes of the law. This is called the administrative definition of over-indebtedness.

A key element in/of the administrative definition of over-indebtedness is the official recognition of a debtor's failure to pay a certain debt. That may happen through the courts or by the nature of the claim (Betti et al. 2001). The latter category includes those obligations which can be collected through legal means (forced sale of property, wage attachments and so on) without court procedures. Depending on jurisdiction these items include, for example, taxes, rates, fines, alimony, child maintenance and insurance payments.

A precondition for administrative over-indebtedness is that the creditor will take legal action to collect the debt. Creditors have their own actions, measures and definitions for default before they decide to go to court (Ford 1988). The creditor will normally apply soft measures to enforce payment before initiating legal actions. When an invoice or a loan is left unpaid after the due date the creditors will send a reminder letter and, in most cases, will charge extra interest on the overdue payment. Sometimes they call up the debtor or send another, this time more angry letter. What is relevant here is that the creditors cannot take any serious action (for example garnishing wages, selling property, evicting tenants) before the overdue payment is processed through the courts. The situation changes dramatically after the court has confirmed an unpaid debt.

A key feature of the administrative definition of over-indebtedness is the qualitatively negative change in people's economic conditions once a debt is confirmed through the courts. This is most clearly visible among those who had large debts and large assets before insolvency and among those who face losing their homes. Janet Ford (1988, pp. 109–111), who interviewed 40 households with mortgage arrears in the UK, notes a qualitative change in defaulter conditions after they realized that they could lose their homes. The initial situation of arrears was described with words such as "shock", "panic", "frightened", "scared". According to Ford (1988, p. 129), the borrowers saw their situation not only as difficult but also as qualitatively changed:

By "not paying" they believed they were perceived and judged differently and more harshly, they faced a set of circumstances whose outcomes were unknown and where they had very limited ideas and knowledge as to the best or appropriate course of action. They found it hard to convey their position to others.

The category of most affected debtors includes also misfortune entrepreneurs and investors who risk losing their lifetime achievements in terms of assets and savings. It is important to note, however, that even for poor individuals and households with small debts and no assets the administrative decision to determine payment liability is a qualitative change towards more serious financial difficulties. However, "judgment debt" as such does not amount to insolvency. The process concerning judgment debt is simply a legal determination of payment liability, and does not concern a debtor's ability to pay.

We may assess the relevance of the administrative definition of over-indebtedness by contrasting it with the five criteria for defining over-indebtedness presented in a study carried out for the European Commission (Fondeville et al. 2010):

1. The unit of measurement should be the household because the incomes of individuals are usually pooled within the same household.
2. Indicators need to cover all aspects of households' financial commitments: borrowing for housing purposes, consumer credit, to pay utility bills, to meet rent and mortgage payments and so on.
3. Over-indebtedness implies an inability to meet recurrent expenses, and therefore should be seen as a structural rather than a temporary state.
4. It is not possible to resolve the problem simply by borrowing more.
5. For a household to meet its commitments, it must reduce its expenses substantially or find ways of increasing its income.

As to the first criterion, administrative definition, at first sight, seems to fail the test. The procedures to determine payment defaults concern individuals, not households. However, the consequences of one household member's insolvency affect everyone in the household. The same applies to the second criterion. While the court determines the validity of individual claims, a possible payment default has potential consequences for all the household's financial commitments.

The third criterion recognizes the fact that the term over-indebtedness refers to severe debt problems. That is the case with the administrative definition of over-indebtedness. Consequences of payment default, for example, follow individuals for a long time in terms of default entries in credit reports. They may limit individuals and households' capability to participate in a normal way of life/living for several years even if the overdue payment is subsequently settled (CPEC 2013). The benefit of the administrative definition of over-indebtedness is that it is not necessary to give a definite amount of deficit either in absolute or relative terms to determine a severe debt problem.

The fourth and fifth criteria are fully covered in the administrative definition of over-indebtedness. The consequences of payment default are so severe, including possible loss of home and all other properties, that households are likely to exhaust all options to borrow more money and/or reduce expenses and/or increase incomes to avoid payment default.

MODIFIED ADMINISTRATIVE DEFINITION OF OVER-INDEBTEDNESS

In the following, we will take the administrative definition of over-indebtedness as a starting point while acknowledging five major limitations in this approach. Firstly, as stated earlier, some claims can be collected through forceful measures even if they are not litigated. Secondly, there are also other claims which, before court proceedings, may result in serious consequences for everyday life if they are left unpaid. For example, a household may lose access to water, heating and electricity if utility bills are left unpaid. Disconnecting vital utility services can also have critical consequences, especially in extreme climate conditions. The service providers do not need a court decision to discontinue service delivery. The same goes for phone lines and internet subscriptions (although prepaid options are currently available). In the absence of universal health care patients with serious illnesses may lose their lives if they cannot pay for their vital treatment. This situation can, no doubt, be characterized in terms of over-indebtedness even if there is no court decision to claim back the overdue medical debts.

We may, however, include these instances in an administrative definition of over-indebtedness since consumer law and similar provisions regulate the conditions under which a utility service company can stop their services. Given the compounded nature of default consequences and the regulated procedures to discontinue services it is reasonable to assume that households would not leave these types of claims unpaid as a result of forgetfulness, even if the overdue amount is small.

Thirdly, the consequences of unpaid claims are bound to a specific welfare state and legal context. In some contexts, non-payment can have life-threatening consequences if vital medical treatment is discontinued as a result of payment neglect. That would not be possible in countries providing universal access to health care. The health care providers' practices with regard to unpaid medical debt may not be regulated in consumer law or similar provisions. In addition, many countries provide means-tested social assistance for individuals and/or households with difficulties paying utility and/or medical bills. These practices may be regulated in law or they may be discretionary.

Fourthly, sometimes the negative consequences of indebtedness set in before payment default. People may try to meet their financial obligations to an extent that seriously affects their essential consumption. Take an example of a tenant who gives nearly 90 per cent of her welfare allowance to a landlord to repay overdue rent and to avoid eviction. In that case it would be feasible to agree on a debt/income ratio which could be used as a yardstick analogous to the definition of relative poverty (40, 50 or 60 per cent of median income). Private individuals service their debts with incomes from their work input, entrepreneurial activities or from social security payments. We may try to define over-indebtedness through setting a threshold for debt/income ratio. The definition is valuable in identifying persons/households that are about to live beyond their means. But even this definition would end up in difficulties with very high incomes and debts. In addition, this approach does not fully capture the impact of debt collection procedures.

Finally, we need to consider whether or not over-indebted individuals have positive assets. The strength of over-indebtedness as a social measure is the very fact that it concerns not only income but also wealth. In many cases over-indebtedness indicates that people have negative assets. However, it does not follow from the administrative definition of over-indebtedness that it could be equated with no assets. Under some circumstances people are ready to face debt judgment even if they hold some assets, for example a family home. Many jurisdictions divide debtors in insolvency proceedings into two categories, as will be later discussed, on the basis of whether or not they have any remaining assets.

In the following we will use a modified administrative definition of over-indebtedness. By this definition *over-indebted persons are those who have defaulted on claims which have been confirmed through court and which are collected by creditors – including claims which can be distrained without litigation (for example unpaid taxes) – or which through an administrative regulated process or otherwise lead to serious consequences (for example the household has no electricity, heating or water*). This book is based on the hypothesis that the social consequences of over-indebtedness are related to the qualitative changes taking place when debt collection actions are initiated and/or when the serious consequences covered by the definition set in.

Of course, even using this modified administrative definition of over-indebtedness we need to consider the possibility of false positives and false negatives. False positives would relate to cases where relatively well-off individuals or households (would) end up with payment defaults, for example, as a result of irresponsibility or determined decision not to pay a certain claim (for example alimony or child maintenance). This problem could be avoided by using a narrower legal definition – for example, personal insolvency, debt settlement or debt discharge – as an indicator of over-indebtedness. However, that would create more problems since not all unpaid claims end up being discharged, and not all debtors seek and/or are granted debt settlement.

In any case, payment default, whether caused by lack of funds or lack of motivation to pay, comes with a number of negative consequences for the debtor, including bad credit reports with ensuing problems in getting insurance, renting accommodation or getting a job. In the US, for example, landlords may docket a money judgment which could appear in tenants' credit reports for many years, accruing 12 per cent interest (Desmond 2016). It will be a real barrier to self-reliance and security for those who try to take a step forward and apply for a student loan or purchase a first house, for example.

Payment default as a definition of over-indebtedness may also lead to false negatives. It is possible that there are people struggling with insurmountable debts who never end up in administrative records. The most obvious example is underwater mortgage debtors who have lost all their equity but continue to service their debts in an effort to avoid foreclosure. False negatives may also stem from more unusual circumstances, such as private debts (for example drug debts). Lastly, the problem with an objective measure such as payment default is that the rules governing such procedures, and the policies and practices can vary between countries, and perhaps between regions within countries. This topic is further discussed in the next chapter.

Finally, we need to make a distinction between a *definition* of over-indebtedness and an *indicator* of over-indebtedness. For theoretical and analytical purposes, it is imperative to define over-indebtedness. However, as described above, previous research has convincingly demonstrated that there is no single valid definition of over-indebtedness which could be translated into a single quantitative indicator; nor is there a quantitative measure which could effectively capture all the necessary dimensions of over-indebtedness. Over-indebtedness is complex and multi-dimensional, and therefore to measure the quantity and the quality of over-indebtedness multiple indicators must be assessed, collected and analysed.

CREDIT-BASED SOCIAL POLICY

The notion of credit-based social policy adds a new dimension to discussion on the role of welfare states and over-indebtedness. The terms "credit-based social policy" or "asset-based welfare" denote a policy paradigm which emphasizes the regulation and promotion of private assets as a means of social security (Mertens 2017). The paradigm is based on the assumption that the ownership of property and shares acts as a buffer for individuals and households facing social risks, particularly during illness, unemployment and retirement, over their life cycle. The welfare state should then support and incentivize economic behaviour that facilitates ownership and investment in order to protect individuals and households from social risks. Within this paradigm over-indebtedness is a situation which seriously endangers the capacity of personal assets to act as a buffer against social risks.

Traditionally the role of markets in providing social protection has been understood through wages and business income, which are then used as savings, sometimes through private insurances acting as buffers against social risks. In terms of welfare state classification, where social risks are pooled by the state, by employers or in the market, credit-based social policy is connected with the role of private wealth and financial markets. Prasad (2012) adds a new dimension to the role of markets and credit by arguing that differences in debt levels between different countries originate from the compensatory character of credit. In the credit-based paradigm is it believed that credit may also compensate for the lack of life cycle-specific public benefits, such as child allowances or housing benefits, and may serve as an instrument for social mobility when allowing both property investments (homeownership) and human capital investment (educational loans) (Logemann 2012, p. 203).

Credit-based social policy has been pursued to enhance social and political stability, or discipline endorsed to promote neoliberal capitalism (Soederberg 2014). As Harvey (1978, p. 15) already notes: "a worker mortgaged up to the hilt is, for the most part, a pillar of social stability". During times of labour shortages, employers preferred to hire married men with mortgages who were tied down by debt and responsibility. Already the instalment plans used to sell cars and household appliances forced the workers to adjust their lives to the discipline of monthly payments (Ramsay 2017, p. 27). With financial deregulation and economic and political pressure on welfare state finances, homeownership has become an increasingly important tool in risk protection. Mortgages appear as an individual strategy for attaining economic security. Home equity can be used to finance current and future consumption as well as emergency cash and disguised retirement saving (Schwartz 2012, p. 48). During crises, the value of a home can be realized through specific financial vehicles.

Borrowing ideas from Foucault, Lazzarato (2012) argues that a debt-dominated economy has created the "indebted man" who is supposed to learn to exploit credit markets appropriately and develop a way of life, discipline, attitudes and conduct which fits into the logic of the markets. Individuals are expected to take into account the credit scoring technologies and teachings from the financial literacy education movement in their daily lives. According to Lazzarato, debt is not only an economic mechanism but also a technique of "public safety" through which individual and collective subjectivities are governed and controlled. Soederberg (2014) takes a step even further when arguing that capital exploits workers through the credit system, where stagnant wages are compensated with high-cost credit. According to Soederberg the rhetoric of democratization of credit, financial inclusion and consumer protection is used to normalize credit as a disciplining instrument of the neoliberal state. Soederberg has coined the term "debtfare". The debtfare state imposes the market discipline of high-cost credit to the poor and serves the interests of the "poverty industry".

In short, credit-based social policy has three dimensions. Firstly, it is about the use of loans as a means of social policy, for instance, through public loan programmes and repayment subsidies. The idea is to help individuals and households accumulate capital which could be used to face social risks. Secondly, it entails using loans as a substitute for social policy, as is the case when households make use of commercial credit offers in order to obtain social or health care services or when they use credit to finance everyday consumption needs emerging from social risks such as unemployment or work disability. Thirdly, and most importantly for the context of this book, credit-based social policy deals with the rules and regulations concerning consumer credit defaults.

In many respects, our six countries provide interesting avenues to study credit-based social policy. The policies facilitating credit-based social policy can be traced back to the Reagan era in the US and the Thatcher era in the UK. The US has promoted homeownership through mortgage interest deduction and the UK with mortgage interest relief at source (Ford 1988; Mian and Sufi 2015a). In the US, government-sponsored enterprises (GSEs) – such as Fannie Mae (the Federal National Mortgage Association, FNMA), Freddie Mac (the Federal Home Loan Mortgage Corporation, FHLMC) and Ginnie Mae (the Government National Mortgage Association, GNMA) – improved low- and middle-income households' access to homeownership by lowering the cost of mortgages by extending guarantees and building a secondary market for mortgage-backed securities (Fligstein and Goldstein 2012). Most importantly, that happened without any additional burden on the taxpayer at the time. The same holds true for the growing student loans markets in the US which have been accompanied by a gradual reduction in public support for higher education. Instead of trying to fight the massive increase in tuition fees with direct support to higher education institutions, the US has allowed the shift from grants to loans (Quinterno 2012; Williams 2006).

The US welfare state demonstrates that credit may cushion social risks such as unemployment and illness, serving as a "debt safety-net" (Montgomerie 2013; Trumbull 2012). For example, if a worker loses his job but can skip mortgage payment without foreclosure, he can seek work without selling the house. In this case, the mortgage has a feature resembling unemployment insurance (Mian and Sufi 2015a, p. 69). Credit can also compensate for stagnant wages, as the US case demonstrates. In the US, mortgage-credit growth between 2002 and 2005 was negatively correlated with income growth (Mian and Sufi 2015a, p. 79).

Public policies concerning credit access, taxation and debtor protection are central features of the Anglo-liberal welfare state model (Crouch 2009; Hay 2011, 2013; Montgomerie 2013). Also, Germany, the Netherlands and the Nordic countries have a long history in promoting household savings, especially homeownership (Mertens 2017; Poppe 2008; Poppe et al. 2016). It can be also argued that welfare state interventions such as sickness and unemployment insurance have been supporting the use of credit by underwriting potential risks or problems with its use. As Janet Ford (1988, p. 39) observed, sick pay, health care provisions, unemployment benefits and pensions reduce the uncertainties relating to income continuity or the need to set money aside for cases of emergency and make credit a possibility.

As opposed to mortgages and student loans, credit-based social policy has not been actively promoting the use of credit to finance health care (Mertens 2017). However, unlike the health care systems in Europe, the US welfare state does not provide universal coverage. That leaves a gap to be filled through accumulation of medical debt. Given the catastrophic nature of health care costs for the uninsured, medical debt can amount to substantial volumes. In the absence of universal health care or employer-sponsored health care provision, the cost of treatment for many households is too high to be paid out of current incomes, inducing the use of credit and particularly high-limit credit cards. Private consumer spending on health care – which constitutes the main difference between American and European expenditure patterns – is a compensatory feature resulting from an underdeveloped public system of health provision. A series of empirical studies on bankruptcies in the US in the 1980s and 1990s showed that bankruptcy is a middle-class phenomenon representing a pragmatic response to a high debt economy where people have little public support in the event of unemployment or sickness (Ramsay 2017, pp. 31–32). More generally, the use of credit, for example with credit cards, to finance everyday consumption can be seen as a strategy to adapt to social risks which are not covered by the welfare state.

METHOD AND DATA SOURCES

We use a comparative policy analysis to describe how policies pertaining to over-indebtedness, causes of over-indebtedness and consequences of over-indebtedness differ across countries. With regard to data sources we rely mostly on published data and literature from various fields, including legal studies, economics, social epidemiology and comparative welfare state research. A key source of illustrative examples is the 2013 Civic Consulting of the Consumer Policy Evaluation Consortium report (CPEC 2013). This report, produced at the request of the Directorate General Health and Consumers (DG SANCO), included analysis of 277 stakeholder interviews in all European Union (EU) Member States (covering the financial industry, civil society organizations, public authorities and independent experts) and a total of 120 face-to-face interviews with over-indebted households in six countries (France, Hungary, Germany, Slovenia, Spain and the UK). It also involved desk research and analysis of available statistical data; an analysis of specific aspects in selected Member States through country experts; and an EU27 survey of organizations active in addressing instances of over-indebtedness, debt counselling and guidance services.

With regard to debt collection procedures and personal insolvency regimes we rely on the rich, mostly juridical, literature in the field. We also utilize German credit insurance company Euler Hermes' open online database of debt collection systems in 44 countries. The country profiles compiled by the company's debt collecting experts review factors such as collection practices, court proceedings and insolvency proceedings that will impact collection of debts in a country (Euler Hermes 2017).

In studying the causes and consequences of over-indebtedness we would have liked to rely on national or comparative register data. While register data produced for administrative purposes has shortcomings, it does not suffer from self-reporting biases. As a country with a long tradition of public registers, Finland has excellent data sources for conducting social epidemiological studies on over-indebtedness. The availability of excellent registers and the possibility of merging them allows, for example, study of the intergenerational effects of over-indebtedness. Unfortunately, similar registers are not available for all countries. A few previously unpublished examples from the Finnish register studies are given.

2. Falling into over-indebtedness

Before filing for bankruptcy Rembrandt van Rijn was heavily indebted to a number of merchants, some of them his friends, and to an influential politician in Amsterdam. All of his assets were pledged many times over as collateral. The legal framework of *cessio bonorum,* surrender of goods, applied in the city of Amsterdam offered a partial solution to Rembrandt's problems. It is important to note, though, that the *cessio bonorum* was not the only way out of the predicament. Rembrandt could have indentured himself or worked out contractual arrangements to satisfy his creditors. He could also have just left town. In surrendering his possessions, the Desolate Boedelskamer (Chamber of Insolvent Estates) in Amsterdam inventoried all Rembrandt's assets, including his house and enormous art collection, which were sold in the course of the following two years. The creditors received the proceeds from the sale, and most of the remaining debts were discharged (Crenshaw 2006, p. 1). Rembrandt was able to stay in Amsterdam and continue as an artist and earn money through his chosen profession. However, the debts were not completely discharged, and they continued to plague him until the end of his life.

Owing money would not be a problem if creditors did not try to collect it. The very definition of over-indebtedness called upon in this book takes debt collection measures initiated by creditors as a starting point for the analysis. The institution of private property comes with the presumption that the state will guarantee a creditor's right to collect payment from a debtor. In case of default, the creditor may turn to the courts to get his money back (Euler Hermes 2017).

Despite the wide range of nationally unique features, all debt recovery procedures comply with a simple five-stage model (Table 2.1). The *first stage* involves a routine of warnings and requests with deadlines and charges to be covered by the default-debtor (Poppe 2008, p. 18). During this period creditors have their specific practices based on a set number of days, for example 30, 60, 90 days overdue (CPEC 2013, p. 25). This process is associated with stress and sometimes harassment of debtors.

Table 2.1   Five-stage model for falling into over-indebtedness

Stage	Procedure	Actors	Effects on debtor
1.	Routine of requests and warnings	Creditor, debt collectors	Stress, harassment
2.	Court procedures	Court officials, attorneys, debt collectors	Extra costs
3.	Debt collection actions	Enforcement officials	Economic deprivation, homelessness
4.	Entry into personal insolvency process	Court officials, debt counsellors	Possible debt discharge
5.	Official credit records	Credit rating agencies	Loss of credit worthiness, financial and social exclusion

If claims remain unpaid, debtors eventually end up in the court system, being the *second stage* in the process. Public creditors have special authorization and typically run the process themselves according to a simplified and more direct debt recovery routine (Poppe 2008, p. 18). Private creditors such as banks and firms may hire a debt collection agency to do the job. This stage allows, in most cases, the creditor to add up costs for the debtor. Debt recovery has become a lucrative and growing business for many firms, some of which are closely linked to the loan-making industry (we will return to this topic).

Besides debtors and creditors, the actors at the second stage include also court officials. This group comprises those actors that perform various functions under civil law, and includes judges, court clerks, trustees, administrative agencies, lawyers, social workers, debt counsellors and financial education providers. With regard to debtors' leeway the involvement of non-judicial actors and the scope of discretionary powers are of particular interest. Debtors may need professional and low-cost debt counselling to prepare their defence and/or negotiations with the creditor, which are in some cases obliged by law.

The courts scrutinize the claims and evaluate their validity and take action to formally clarify the legally enforceable debts through court judgments, administrative decisions or by debtor consent. The debtor can file complaints, but most often there is not much to do. That is the time when over-indebtedness is legally confirmed.

Once a judgment is given by the court, the creditor, in the *third stage,* will take action to collect the debt. Debt collection takes various forms depending on the jurisdiction. The creditor may take the claim to the local enforcement officer who is authorized to distrain property, movables and income, and carry out forced sales and wage deductions (Poppe 2008, p. 18). Such action results in economic deprivation among debtors. Depending on the type of clarification, the debtor has instituted routines for making complaints about such steps. However, the reality for many default-debtors is that they have complicated problems and multiple claims against them, such as credit card debts, taxes, fines and child maintenance arrears. This means that they may have to deal not only with the "ordinary" enforcement officer but also a number of other authorities with the right to make distrainments (Poppe 2008, p. 18). Complicated debt problems are demanding also for the different creditors and the courts, which, for example, may have to combine several wage deductions and still make sure they leave the default-debtors with sufficient means for daily needs.

The first three stages concern all debtors who fail to pay their debts in time. The *fourth stage* concerns only those default-debtors who enter the personal insolvency process. This may end in debt settlement or debt discharge, as will be illustrated below. In any case, the debtor will greatly benefit from the help of a qualified debt counsellor in navigating through this process successfully. In describing this stage of over-indebtedness, we may rely on the rich literature on comparative personal insolvency law (for example Niemi-Kiesiläinen 1999; Niemi-Kiesiläinen et al. 2003; Ramsay 2017).

The *fifth and final stage* of over-indebtedness process concerns the consequences of default in terms of official credit records. The rules and regulations concerning the use of payment default records may have grave consequences for the concerned individuals. Public information on recorded payment default may prevent people from getting loans, insurance, phone and internet connections, rented apartments or houses and jobs in the future. In short, loss of credit worthiness may result in economic and social exclusion. Unfortunately, there is very little comparative literature on the topic. This is a major shortcoming in the current knowledge.

TYPES AND VOLUMES OF DEBTS

As stated above modern society rests upon the institution of consumer credit as a vehicle for creating employment and economic growth (Poppe 2008, p. 30). The issue of private debt is closely related to innovations and liberalization policies in finance reaching back a few decades. Households and individuals may end up in debt problems through a range of payment types, some of which are treated differently in debt collection procedures. The payment types relate to all items they consume, from daily groceries to housing loans. Public liabilities such as taxes, fines and fees for the use of public services are more easily enforceable than private debts. The same goes for damage payments and insurance payments.

While credit contracts and their utilization vary greatly across countries, some general trends are clearly visible. In the 1980s, credit cards became a major source of default among consumers in the US (Caplovitz 1967; Ford 1988). At the time, close-ended loans were largely replaced by open-ended credit as the dominant form of consumer debt (Poppe 2008, p. 30). Credit cards and payment cards with account overdraft features allowed multiple purchases by instalment without having to apply for credit each time. Without negotiating credit for all single deliveries of goods or services, credit cards provided people with immediate access to credit.

When evaluating a default-debtor's position in debt collection, we need to consider that different creditors react differently to defaults. For example, while unsecured debts tend to be subject to aggressive debt collection routines, loans against collateral – normally the largest claims – often involve more relaxed enforcement practices. Ford (1988, pp. 125, 150–152, 165) observed already in the 1980s that mortgage creditors like building societies typically react late upon default, and that households facing financial problems therefore tend to pay other, less important debts before mortgage payments. Poppe (2008) detected a similar pattern in Norway. A contrasting experience is derived from a large European study of over-indebtedness. A stakeholder from the Netherlands reported an aggressive debt collection practice of unsecured debts:

> Especially private corporations (not housing or health insurance) are much more aggressive. They sometimes even threat[en] people that they will be evicted when they do not pay for the telephone bill (that is entirely impossible but when you tell this to people involved they are inclined to believe it). (CPEC 2013, p. 201)

Besides credit cards, today's credit markets present households with choices among hundreds of products and product variations offered by thousands of lenders. In the credit market the households combine high-frequency and lower-stakes decisions (e.g. credit card use) with low-frequency and high-stakes decisions (Kilborn 2005). Mortgages feature most prominently in the later category, while the other types are student loans and vehicle loans. Unlike the other key consumer credit markets, mortgages and vehicle loans are collateralized.

Mortgages account for the bulk of household borrowing in OECD countries (André 2016). Different types of mortgage contracts (for example fixed vs. variable rates, local vs. foreign currency, interest-only vs. amortizing) entail different kinds of risks for households. There is a strong association between changes in housing prices and in the volume of household debt. This is obvious, since buying dwellings is the main motive for household borrowing, and households are willing to take out substantial loans to finance the purchase of a house or an apartment. The causality runs both ways. When housing prices go up, households take out bigger loans. This is possible since the higher prices also increase the value of collateral which can be used to obtain credit. Simultaneously, improved access to credit, as a result of lower interest rates or loosening of borrowing constraints, allows households to bid for more expensive homes. As the supply of housing is inelastic in many markets, housing prices go up.

Of course, outstanding debt is not the only measure of economic importance. For instance, total borrowing costs also matter. The problem is that the credit markets, at least in the US, are missing several rungs in the lending ladder between credit cards (which tend to top out around 30 per cent annual percentage rate [APR] for subprime borrowers) and the triple-digit APR small-money products (Kilborn 2005). The gaps are not only striking for interest rates but also for maturities. Credit cards are most often structured as open-ended lines of credit with modest minimum monthly payments, but the maturities for other small-money products such as payday loans are always quite short.

Previous research has demonstrated that the use of unsecured credit is positively associated with the likelihood of arrears, while there is no direct relationship between levels of mortgage borrowing and levels of arrears. In the field of consumer debt, CPEC (2013, p. 93) found a significant positive correlation between the level of consumer debt outstanding at the aggregate level and the frequency of arrears on hire purchase or other loans.

Certain types of debts that are backed up with particularly hard penalties still hold a unique position in debt collection. For example, failing to pay maintenance was punished with forced labour in Norway as late as 1955, and in the UK, those who defaulted on rates payments risked imprisonment in the 1980s (Poppe 2008, p. 18). In the US, those who do not meet their child maintenance obligations or fail to pay criminal justice debt are still at risk of imprisonment (Kim et al. 2015).

Child maintenance debts are a problem in all countries, but especially so in the US. Despite a range of enforcement actions – including suspension of driving licence, denying professional licence and incarceration – the arrears have been increasing since the national child support programme began in 1975 (Kim et al. 2015). The arrears carry significant interest, which reduces non-custodial parents' compliance with ongoing child support obligations and discourages employment. A study on long-time patterns in child support arrears in Wisconsin showed that more than half of the non-custodial parents had arrears and as many as 24 per cent of the parents had a continuous increase in arrears. In many US states parents with payment obligations are discouraged against child support payments which do not reach their children if the non-resident parent receives social assistance. This practice is applied also in countries like Finland and Germany. The public authorities do not pass the child support to the parent with care of the child or they deduct the payment from social assistance (Skinner et al. 2017). The UK is one of the few countries where the child support system is disentangled from other social transfer systems.

Also, other types of private debts such as unpaid medical bills, car payments and payday loans may lead to involvement in the criminal justice system in the US if the creditor or a debt collector bypasses the bankruptcy court and takes the debtor straight to the civil court. In case the debtor fails to show up, or if the judge deems that the debtor is "wilfully" not paying the debt, the judge may write a warrant for the debtor's arrest on a charge of contempt of court (Hager 2015). In a process known as "pay or stay" the debtor is then held in jail until he or she posts bond or pays the debt. Debtors' prison also applies to criminal justice financial obligations, which consists of three sub-categories. Firstly, it includes fines, that is, monetary penalties imposed as a condition of a sentence (for example a traffic ticket). Secondly, this category consists of various fees, for example: jail book-in fees, bail investigation fees, public defender application fees, drug testing fees, DNA testing fees, jail per diem rates for pre-trial detention, court costs, felony surcharges, or public defender recoupment fees. Thirdly, restitution made to the victim or victims for personal or property damage is included in the category of criminal justice financial obligation. As many as 41 states in the US bill the costs of imprisonment to inmates, and 44 states bill for parole and probation.

Within the group of unsecured debts, it is useful to distinguish commercial and non-commercial debts. Commercial creditors (for example credit card companies, mortgage lenders) are most visible in payment default proceedings. However, some of the non-commercial claims – such as taxes, fines, tort claims, alimony and child support claims or student loans – do not need judgments before they can be collected for example through wage garnishment. This group also includes informal credit or loans from family members, friends or employers, which seldom cause over-indebtedness (CPEC 2013, p. 150).

Unsecured commercial creditors are also a heterogeneous group. It includes traditional credit card companies together with providers of easy to obtain but high-cost financial products such as payday or SMS loans and non-usurious credit from unregulated lenders (CPEC 2013, p. 150). While the amounts of these loans are much lower than for mortgages, they are concentrated in the lower income categories of households, where default rates can be high (Kilborn 2005). By looking at the types and level of commitment we may evaluate both the total debt load and the profile of payment difficulties (Table 2.2). Despite differences between different types of debt, in principle they engender a similar response and a similar pattern of management irrespective of their specific form (Ford 1988, p. 9).

Table 2.2   Combined debt load and payment difficulties

	Type of commitment	Possible consequence if commitment left unpaid
Borrowing		
secured	Mortgage, car loans with vehicle as collateral	Loss of house or apartment, loss of vehicle
unsecured	Credit cards, payday loans	No money for basic commodities such as food and clothes
Other commitments	Utility bills, rents	Loss of electricity, disconnected phone line, eviction
Total effect	Combined debt load	Combined payment difficulties

Source: Developed from CPEC (2013, p. 29).

DEBT COLLECTORS

As described above, many creditors routinely use debt collectors if the debt remains unpaid beyond a certain time. That includes both overdue debts which are not confirmed through courts and debts which are processed through courts. Most often debt collectors work for debt-collection agencies, while some operate independently and some are attorneys (Fontinelle 2017). Debt collectors have two different business models. They can act as middlemen, collecting delinquent debts that are due past a stipulated timeframe and remitting them to the original creditor. The debt collector will keep as a collection fee a substantial percentage, typically 25–45 per cent, of the amount collected. In the second model the agencies buy debts from the original creditor, usually in packages of numerous accounts with similar features, and then will keep everything they collect. In these cases, the original creditor has determined that they are unlikely to get payment and will cut their losses by selling the debt to a debt buyer.

In both business models the debt collectors will use all available means to collect the debt, since the more they recover, the more they earn. They use letters and phone calls to reach delinquent borrowers, trying to convince them to pay (Fontinelle 2017). Debt collectors sometimes use inexpedient methods such as calling the debtor any hour of the day, even when children are sleeping, telling employers and neighbours about the problems, using illegal contracts to "settle" the controversies and exer-cising physical violence (Poppe 2008, p. 45). Poppe reported that in Norway several of his 20 informants had experienced money collectors appearing on their doorsteps, as well as unpleasant meetings with the creditor's side, including interrogation-like situations where they were outnumbered by representatives of the opposing party or challenged by friendly and unfriendly negotiators in the same room. Dominy and Kempson (2003) indicate that in the UK a variety of methods are in use to maximize success rates in specified default-debtor segments, and that protective legislation is necessary if acceptable collection practices are to be ensured.

The debt packages sold to debt collectors fall into three categories: accounts that are not that old and that no other collector has worked on yet; accounts that are quite old and that other collectors have failed to collect on; and accounts that fall somewhere in between (Fontinelle 2017). The type of the debt may also influence the price. Of all those with credit files in the US, 35 per cent had an account in collection in 2013, with an average of 5178 US dollars (Ratcliffe et al. 2014). The fact that many of these accounts were owned by specialized third-party collectors that purchase debts from originators or from other collectors poses an abundance of unanswered questions on market structure, contracting and the effects of collection practices and policies on consumer welfare (Fedaseyeu and Hunt 2014). In 2000, the government of Finland sold 76 000 individual debts dating back from the economic recession in the early 1990s to two debt collection agencies at only 5 per cent of the debts' book value.

Debt collectors use computer software, databanks and private investigators to track down debtors who have gone underground (Fontinelle 2017). They also search for a debtor's assets, such as bank and brokerage accounts and real estate, to determine the debtor's ability to repay. They may also threaten to report delinquent debts to credit bureaus to encourage consumers to pay, knowing that delinquent debts can do serious damage to a consumer's credit score. If there is already a court judgment against the debtors, the collector may place levies on bank accounts or motor vehicles, garnish wages, place a lien on property or force the sale of an asset.

Debt collectors' practices are mitigated by the provisions which protect the default-debtors from debt collectors' most outrageous behaviour, be they middlemen or owners of debts. The provisions concern, for example, limitations as to what and how much of debtor's possessions and income can be accessed. The general rule is that default-debtors are allowed to keep as much income as is necessary to meet an adequate subsistence level, and to hold on to possessions that are required to cover basic needs (Poppe 2008, p. 19). As Poppe notes, the problem is that the terms "adequate subsistence levels" and "basic needs" are debatable. Some countries (but not all) have fixed income thresholds in debt recovery through wage garnishments. The situation is even more complex when it comes to debt settlement agreements (see below), where factors such as the default-debtor's housing expenses, the number of people living in the household and the extent to which they may have extra income without the need to renegotiate the agreement are considered.

As for a debtor's property, the general rule is that it must be put on sale and be sold to the benefit of the creditors. A forced sale of property is a result of a long process which involves careful economic and judicial considerations with warnings and opportunities to protest and negotiate. Special provisions concern the forced sale of a default-debtor's home (also called fire sale). The family is sometimes entitled to a replacement arranged by the municipality. The clauses protecting the default-debtor's rights are, however, strictly limited and do not give much leeway. Low-income and low-educated debtors may be subject to harsher debt collection procedures since they do not understand the system, are unable to anticipate the steps taken against them and cannot seek refuge in the remedies included in the legislation and industry codes of good debt collection practices (Caplovitz 1967; CPEC 2013).

There is evidence that debt collectors actually harass consumers. In the US the Federal Trade Commission (FTC) gets more complaints about debt collectors than about any other industry (Federal Trade Commission 2017). The agency enforces the Fair Debt Collection Practices Act (FDCPA), which prohibits deceptive, unfair and abusive debt collection practices. In 2017 the FTC announced that it had sued over 30 debt collection companies for violating the law, banning some from the business and making them pay steep financial penalties. According to the FTC (2017):

> Some collectors harass and threaten consumers, demand larger payments than the law allows, refuse to verify disputed debts, and disclose debts to consumers' employers, co-workers, family members, and friends. Debt collection abuses cause harms that financially vulnerable consumers can ill afford. Many consumers pay collectors money they do not owe and fall deeper into debt, while others suffer invasions of their privacy, job loss, and domestic instability.

Debt collection has implications far beyond individual debtor–creditor relationships as it is punitive by nature and linked to mechanisms that over time may lead to financial exclusion (Poppe 2008, p. 46). People with poor payment records increasingly are excluded from mainstream credit offers and they turn to subprime and sub-subprime markets, including unlicensed moneylenders and criminal circles. That not only leads to more expensive credit but also to poorer consumer protection and higher risks for additional financial troubles. Unpaid debts also affect other areas of services such as banking, insurance, housing and job markets. Banks may close down overdrawn accounts or deny people regular savings accounts or transaction accounts due to bad credit histories. That will lead to expensive and tedious bill paying and makes it difficult to get a job, furnish a home, or get a plan for old age through life insurance and pension savings (CPEC 2013, p. 189; Poppe 2008, p. 46; Ford 1988, p. 137). Debt collection may also end up in determination of insolvency if the debtor cannot pay the claims due to lack of income and assets. Insolvency is fortunately not the ultimate stage in the process.

DEBT SETTLEMENT OR DISCHARGE

A debt settlement or a consumer bankruptcy is a process which, under certain conditions, entails the possibility of a financial fresh start via coercive cancellation of claims. As opposed to the process described above where a single claim is confirmed through the courts, debt settlement or direct debt discharge does not concern a single claim but instead all the debtor's financial commitments. The aim of the process is twofold: to provide a financial fresh start for honest, insolvent, non-business individuals; and to regulate the collection and distribution of the debtor's (non-exempt) assets and/or earnings. Since most of the cases yield few or no proceeds for distribution among creditors, the first goal has clearly more practical importance (Heuer 2013). Debt settlement is a major factor in defining over-indebtedness outcomes both at individual and societal level. However, irrespective of jurisdiction, not all over-indebted individuals/households can or will seek debt settlement.

Legally, debt discharge signifies an intrusion of welfare policies into private/civil law by enforcing a doctrine of "social force majeure" (Wilhelmsson 1990; Niemi-Kiesiläinen 2003). In terms of public policy, debt discharge tackles a social problem not in terms of redistribution but in terms of regulation in the private sphere. It is at the core of credit-based social policy, where the state uses credit as a means to pool social risks – in this case the unintended consequences of risk pooling through credit. Over-indebtedness covers a large variety of social risks associated with debt problems, where debt discharge includes a solution without committing public funds.

Heuer (2013) divides the chameleonic history of personal bankruptcy and the history of debt collection into three phases. The term "bankruptcy" is derived from the Latin words *banca* (bench) and *rupta* (broken). It originated in medieval Italy, where it referred to a supposed practice of breaking non-paying merchants' benches in outdoor markets in order to destroy their trading places. However, important features of consumer bankruptcy are that the debtor can initiate the process and that discharge of debts can also be instituted against the creditor's will. In some jurisdictions bankruptcy and insolvency have technically distinct legal meanings. Since this is not a legal text the terms "bankruptcy" and "insolvency" are used interchangeably throughout.

In the first phase of bankruptcy law history the action focused on the collection of debts from defaulting debtors, and subjected debtors to severe punishments, for example public humiliation, the loss of civil and political rights, banishment, imprisonment, debt bondage, mutilation or the death penalty. The aim was to assert the principles of personal responsibility, reciprocity and *Pacta sunt servanda* (agreements must be kept). The first English bankruptcy acts of 1542 and 1570, among the early "modern" bankruptcy laws, treated defaulting debtors as quasi-criminals. The laws were essentially tools for debt collection in the hands of creditors; as Heuer (2013) states, "relief was not for debtors, but from debtors".

Only during the second phase did bankruptcy laws begin to balance the interests of creditors and debtors in business and commercial matters (Heuer 2013). Consequently, the laws became less punitive and acknowledged that the reorganization of an insolvent debtor might also be more profitable for creditors than the exclusive focus on debt collection. Debt discharge was first introduced in English bankruptcy law in the early 18th century, although the discharge was originally only an element of a "carrot and stick" policy – rewarding debtors for cooperation with debt relief while threatening "uncooperative" debtors with the death penalty. In the 19th and early 20th century, new bankruptcy systems following the English legal tradition allowed debtors to initiate bankruptcy proceedings themselves and made debt relief available for non-traders. However, even in the Anglo-Saxon countries bankruptcy was predominantly used for companies and not for consumers.

During the last few decades personal bankruptcy laws have undergone yet another transformation into social and consumer policy instruments that are aimed to tackle the new social risk of consumer over-indebtedness (Ramsay 2017). According to Heuer (2013) the transformation in the third phase of bankruptcy law history has followed two paths. The Anglo-Saxon countries (such as England/Wales, Scotland, Australia, New Zealand, Canada and the US) have amended their established personal bankruptcy laws to adapt them to meet the challenges of over-indebtedness in the modern consumer markets. Previously, personal bankruptcy and debt discharge were not available to private debtors outside the Anglo-Saxon countries. However, several European countries began to introduce consumer debt relief provisions as a new legal instrument, especially in the 1990s (Norway and Finland in 1993, Sweden 1994, Austria 1993/95, Germany 1994/99, the Netherlands 1998, Belgium 1998/99, France 1998/99). This development was prompted by banking crises in the Nordic countries (Kiander and Vartia 2011), while in Germany the adjustment to reunification acted as a background factor for new bankruptcy laws. These countries considered the US idea of straight discharge but rejected it. Instead all reforms included significant repayment periods before discharge was permissible (Ramsay 2017, p. 5).

The debt settlement procedure aims to determine debtors' payment capacity. Debtors fall into two distinct categories. The assets and earnings of "no income, no assets" (NINA) debtors are so low that they are exempt from collection. Debtors in the second category can pay at least part of their creditors' claims. Creditors can also be divided into two groups. The first group consists of those whose claims are secured by collateral in the debtor's property (secured creditors), while those with no security for their claims on the debtor's property (unsecured creditors) form the second group. Consumer bankruptcy concerns mainly unsecured creditors and does not alter creditors' rights in collateral, which continue during and after bankruptcy. However, debt settlement may also concern secured creditors if the collateral is a family home (Heuer 2013).

The debt settlement process is initiated either by a petition from the debtor or, if allowed, from a creditor. The petition must meet certain personal and financial preconditions (for example regarding the debtor's location, debt levels, asset levels, number of creditors, formation and duration of debt problems) and might involve an access screening (that is, individual examination of the debtor's personal and economic situation). While the petition is processed a stay of (individual) debt enforcement might come into effect, easing the debtors' situation vis-à-vis creditors. In some jurisdictions debt settlement and consumer bankruptcy may subject the debtors to educational and behavioural obligations – financial education lessons, labour market obligations (for example searching employment) or credit market obligations (for example not obtaining credit) – or disqualifications and restrictions, be they economic (such as not managing a company), political (not voting or holding elected office) or civil (not leaving the country) (Heuer 2013). The process usually concludes with partial or full debt discharge, which can be automatic, discretionary or conditional.

As opposed to business debt settlements and bankruptcies, consumer bankruptcy is a "small stakes game" that is more administrative than legal or adversarial in nature (Heuer 2013). Private persons' bankruptcy estates very seldom have enough funds to cover the process which would leave expenses for the creditors. During economic crises, many small business owners are dragged into insurmountable financial problems when they go bankrupt. For them the only way to manage debts is through voluntary or enforced debt settlement.

Debt settlement is not an easy way out of debt problems. As will be demonstrated in detail below, a number of administrative units and statutory services have typically been called upon to provide various types of solutions to financial problems before debt settlement is granted (Poppe 2008, p. 21). The sight of complex legal proceedings in the middle of financial problems easily leads private individuals into a quagmire. Depending on country, the debtor has a number of options, ranging from private debt advisors to statutory public services, to find debt counselling. Debt counsellors have an established, sometimes legislated position in handling default-debtors. They may not only give advice to debtors on which options to rely on; they may also carry out extrajudicial negotiations with the creditors to try to establish voluntary repayment schemes. Private advisors, including lawyer services, come with substantial costs. However, municipal, NGO-based or church-based free of charge options may be stigmatizing.

PERSONAL INSOLVENCY REGIMES

As in Rembrandt's time the normative constraints with regard to a default-debtor's treatment are embedded in historic time and space, and appear as more or less appropriate relative to the social environments in which they claim validity (Poppe 2008, p. 12). By analysing the rules, aims and contexts of consumer over-indebtedness scholars have tried, especially after the Global economic crisis of 2008, to identify distinct models of consumer debt relief (Niemi-Kiesiläinen 1999, 2003; Kilborn 2005; Heuer 2013; Ramsay 2017). The efforts have resulted in somewhat contradictory classifications regarding the number of debt relief models and the allocation of national systems to these models.

A personal insolvency regime tries to balance the rights of creditors and individual debtors in case of insolvency. The regime consists of features which address:

- the provisions for triggering personal insolvency proceedings;
- whether debtors and/or creditors can initiate the proceedings;
- treatment of different creditors;
- treatment of different types of debt (for example, unsecured and secured);
- duration of possible debt settlement;
- provisions for debt discharge;
- payment obligations and schedules; and
- the time limitations for enforcement of judgment debts.

Heuer (2013) has identified three sets of questions regarding a regime's main aim of consumer bankruptcy for insolvent consumers (see also Ramsay 2017, p. 8). The first questions concern the eligibility of debtors to have a fresh start. These refer to restricting and facilitating conditions for consumer bankruptcy: the prevention of bankruptcy misuse; educational and behavioural obligations for debtors; debtor disqualifications and restrictions; debtor protection; and support for NINA debtors. The second set of questions concern the scope of the fresh start, namely what is discharged. The third set of questions concern the timing of the fresh start and refer to the duration of bankruptcy.

On the basis of these dimensions Heuer has constructed a model of four consumer bankruptcy regimes (Table 2.3). The United States represents a market model of consumer bankruptcy systems which allows quick discharge of contractual debts but excludes many claims from non-commercial/reluctant creditors from the discharge (for example student debts). Heuer uses the term "market model" to describe the underlying assumption of consumer bankruptcy discharge as a means of risk allocation in the credit market that shifts the risk and costs of default from debtors to creditors in order to increase market efficiency.

Table 2.3 Four types of personal insolvency regimes

	Focus on debtor–creditor relations	Focus on debtor–society relations
Focus on debtor	Liability model (Germany, Netherlands)	Mercy model (Finland, Norway)
Focus on creditor or society	Market model (US)	Restrictions model (UK)

Source: Heuer (2013).

England/Wales and Scotland share several features with the market model – for example a rather short duration of bankruptcy (one to three years) – but they also have several economic, political and civil disqualifications and restrictions for debtors during and after bankruptcy. Heuer calls the model "restrictive" while noting that the system exhibits notions of protecting society from debtors and upholding public order.

Germany represents the liability model of consumer bankruptcy system, which is characterized by long payment periods (six years) and includes a number of educational and behavioural obligations for debtors, and control rights for creditors. This model resembles the market model from the view of consumer over-indebtedness as an economic phenomenon, but it is directly opposed to the market model in that it emphasizes the debtor's responsibility for debt repayment (not the creditor's responsibility for making informed lending decisions) and aims to increase payments to the creditor. The Netherlands, with restricted access to debt discharge, can be also included in this model (Klein 2016; Ramsay 2017).

Heuer calls the fourth type the "mercy model", claiming that in this model the debtors are at the mercy of bankruptcy officials. In this model, represented for example by Finland and Norway, bankruptcy laws are driven by social-political notions of "deservingness" and focus on the needs and abilities of debtors. The needs are evaluated by bankruptcy officials who have broad discretionary powers to shape the initiation, course, duration and outcome of debt relief proceedings.

The difference between the US and continental tradition is aptly described in a Swedish government report which studied efficient ways to offer fresh starts for over-indebted entrepreneurs:

> In the US system, writing off liabilities is regarded as an efficient way to distribute risks. Over-indebtedness is seen as a market failure and is explained as a failure of the market to assess the risks. With this approach, it is logical to regard debt restructuring as a means of efficiently tackling problems of over-indebtedness so as to enable the individual to rapidly return to the market as a consumer and borrower. It has been pointed out that in Europe over-indebtedness is regarded as a social or moral problem and that the debtor is expected to bear more of the risk. (SOU 2014)

In the following section we will review central features of debt collection and personal insolvency regimes in the six countries, with the emphasis on their impact on the debtor.

The United States

In the US the debt collection system is complicated by the federal structure consisting of 50 states and one federal district (Washington, DC), each characterized by specific rules and specific courts (Euler Hermes 2017). Payments are due normally within 28 days. Late payment interest may be charged to the debtor up to the legal rate of interest allowed by the state in which the debtor resides. The creditor cannot legally charge collection costs without a prior agreement signed by the debtor authorizing such charges.

Despite the US's pioneering role in instalment payment schemes, contractual agreements aimed at preserving the creditor's ownership over goods until the related invoice has been paid in full no longer exist in the US. Cheques are still the most common payment instrument in the US. Legal dunning (communication with relevant parties to ensure the collection of payment) starts with a registered Demand Letter recalling the debtor's obligation to pay the principal, together with late payment interest. Before starting legal proceedings against a debtor, the creditor assesses the debtor's assets and solvency status.

Provided that the debt is certain and undisputed, the creditor may first file an application for summary judgment. Ordinary legal action usually commences when amicable collection attempts have failed (Euler Hermes 2017). The creditor would file a claim with the court prior to serving summons to the debtor. The debtor would then be given 30 days (in most jurisdictions) to raise a defence. Even if they do not dispute the claim, it could take up to a year, depending on the jurisdiction and the staffing available, before a default judgment is given.

The available methods for a judgment debt collection depend on the type of debt. They also vary from state to state. Judgment creditors normally first will go after debtors' pay cheque through wage attachment or wage garnishment (Reiter 2017). To attach a debtor's wages, a judgment creditor obtains authorization from the court in a document usually called a writ. Under this authorization, the judgment creditor directs the sheriff to seize a portion of the debtor's wages. The sheriff in turn notifies the employer of the attachment, and the employer notifies the debtor. During the process the employer sends the amount withheld each pay period to the sheriff, who deducts his or her expenses and sends the balance to the judgment creditor (Reiter 2017). Federal law allows the judgment creditor to take up to 25 per cent of net earnings or the amount by which the debtor's weekly net earnings exceed 30 times the federal minimum wage. In cases of child support up to 50 per cent of wages may be taken to pay support, while the Internal Revenue Service (IRS) can take up to 100 per cent of wages to pay income taxes. The debtor can object to the wage attachment by requesting a court hearing. In some states, the attachment cannot begin until after the hearing, unless the debtor gives up the right to a hearing (Reiter 2017).

Judgment creditors can also use property lien. In about half the states, a judgment entered against a debtor automatically creates a lien on the real property the debtor owns in the county where the judgment was obtained (Reiter 2017). In the rest of the states, the creditor must record the judgment with the county, and then the recorded judgment creates a lien on the debtor's real property. Liens are in force from a few to several years. Once the judgment creditor has a lien on a debtor's property, the creditor can safely anticipate payment. When the debtor sells or re-finances the property, title must be cleared – that is, all liens must be removed by paying the lienholder – before the deal can be closed (Reiter 2017).

Instead of waiting for the debtor to sell the property, the creditor arranges for a public sale from which the creditor is paid out of the proceeds. Every state has declared certain property as "exempt", meaning it is off-limits to judgment creditors (Reiter 2017). If the property is exempt, the creditor cannot sell the property. However, creditors usually want to avoid the expense and trouble of a public sale. This is especially true if the creditor will not get much money through the sale by the order according to which payments are made (first any mortgage holder, government taxing authority or other creditor who placed a lien on the property before the judgment creditor).

In addition, a judgment creditor can get a "writ of execution" from the court and go after a debtor's personal property by instructing the sheriff or marshal to "levy" on it (Reiter 2017). This means that the officer takes the property or instructs the holder of the property to turn it over to the officer. As a next step the sheriff or marshal sells it at public auction and applies the proceeds to the debt. In the case of a bank account, the amount taken from debtor's account is applied to the debt. An assignment order lets creditors go after property the debtor owns that cannot be subject to a levy, such as an anticipated tax refund, the loan value of premature life insurance or an annuity policy.

As a country with common law tradition the US represents the so-called old system of consumer insolvency which has, since the mid-19th century, recognized the possibility of non-traders discharging debts (Ramsay 2017, p. 4). The US Bankruptcy Code, dating back to 1938, includes specific procedures for companies (Chapter 11), family farmers and fishermen (Chapter 12) as well as for individual wage earners (Chapters 7 and 13), all with specific reorganization options. By allowing two avenues for personal bankruptcy the US system is aimed at: protecting debtors from the accidents of life (unemployment, divorce, medical problems); avoiding undue burden on the social welfare system; and preserving the incentive for debtors to work and add value to society. Creditors tended to criticize the system as "unfair" since it did not make demands on debtors to abide by the "norm" (Kilborn 2005). More recently the situation has changed with new obligations for debtors in many jurisdictions.

Debtors who are not able to honour their debts – not even making the minimum payments – have two options in the US. They may file for Chapter 7 bankruptcy and discharge those obligations, or they may simply skip a payment and become delinquent on debt. The options are referred to as formal and informal default, respectively. Before filing for bankruptcy, households typically go through delinquency for 30 to 120 days. During delinquency debt collectors can garnish typically up to 25 per cent of wages and, depending on the state, the last 1000 dollars of a bank account if exempt. Creditors cannot garnish income from welfare. Bankruptcy stops wage garnishment immediately, and at the end of the process debts are discharged. However, the process is not available to everyone: the household must have some resources, typically at least 1000 dollars, to pay fees and sometimes hire a lawyer.

The overwhelming majority of consumer bankruptcy cases in the US pass through Chapter 7 of the code. This process consists of three simple and largely administrative steps which are usually processed within three months: (1) the debtor's filing of a petition for relief and detailed financial information; (2) the debtor's meeting with a trustee to answer questions about the debtor's financial situation; and (3) the trustee's filing of a report of "no available assets" and entry of a judgment soon thereafter discharging the debtor from most unpaid debts.

Chapter 7 of the Bankruptcy Code provides for "liquidation", that is, the sale of a debtor's non-exempt property and the distribution of the proceeds to creditors. The primary purpose of bankruptcy is to discharge certain debts to give an honest individual debtor a fresh start. In a Chapter 7 bankruptcy case the bankruptcy trustee gathers and sells the debtor's non-exempt assets and uses the proceeds of such assets to pay holders of claims (creditors) in accordance with the provisions of the Bankruptcy Code.

As a result of filing Chapter 7, the overwhelming majority of US consumer debtors dedicate none of their future income to paying their debts. Debtors need not give another thought to the process that led them into and out of over-indebtedness after filing and meeting with the trustee once (Kilborn 2005). This notable model in the US is also highlighted in the marketing of non-recourse loans in many US states. They allow households in negative equity to escape debt, which is much more difficult in most other OECD countries. As opposed to a non-recourse loan, a recourse loan permits a lender to seek financial damages if the borrower fails to pay the liability, and if the value of the underlying asset is not enough to cover it. A recourse loan allows the lender to go after the debtor's assets that were not used as loan collateral in case of default.

Provisions added to the code in 2005 were aimed at limiting the use of Chapter 7 only for those who truly cannot pay their debts. The first step is simple: if a debtor's current monthly income is less than the median income for their household size, the debtor can file for Chapter 7. If the income exceeds median, the debtor must pass a complex means test which aims to determine if the debtor's income left over after paying the "allowed" monthly expenses is enough to pay off at least a portion of unsecured debts. As a step to prevent strategic bankruptcies the law stipulates that a debtor cannot file for Chapter 7 if, within 180 days before filing, he or she has received counselling from an approved credit counselling agency, either individually or in a group briefing. If a debt management plan is developed during required credit counselling, it must be filed with the court.

Filing a petition under Chapter 7 "automatically stays" (stops) most collection actions against the debtor or the debtor's property. As long as the stay is in effect, creditors generally may not initiate or continue lawsuits, wage garnishments or even telephone calls demanding payments. Commencement of a bankruptcy case creates an "estate". The estate technically becomes the temporary legal owner of all the debtor's property. It consists of all legal or equitable interests of the debtor in property as of the commencement of the case, including property owned or held by another person if the debtor has an interest in the property.

Many states have legislated limitations (statute of limitations) to stop lawsuits from collecting on a debt after some time, typically between three and six years, which also gives an incentive for informal default. With regard to credit card debts, the contracts normally have a penalty rate, which increases the costs of informal default; but households may be able to renegotiate that debt with lenders. After the debtor has been delinquent for some time, the federal banking regulations compel the credit card companies to "charge off" the credit. The companies can count the sale of overdue debts to third-party collection agencies as assets for capital requirements. The debt can be then resold from third parties to buyers of distressed debt. A study by the FTC showed that 68 per cent of debts which had been charged off were less than three years old and 71.5 per cent were for less than 1000 dollars (Federal Trade Commission 2017). About 50 per cent of the debts had been sent to a collector, on average with a price of 4 cents for a dollar.

As opposed to Chapter 7, Chapter 13 of the Bankruptcy Code allows the debtor with regular income to keep property and pay debts (or part of them) over time, usually three to five years. In many US states mortgage lenders can claim borrowers' financial assets when the collateral falls short of the loan balance. Chapter 13 is regulated in bankruptcy law but it resembles debt settlement. Approximately one-third of all consumer bankruptcy cases are filed under Chapter 13. However, the law vests broad discretion in the bankruptcy court to reject "wage-earner" payment plans that propose "insufficient" payments to creditors. The code requires Chapter 13 debtors to propose a payment plan in "good faith" and to devote all of their "disposable income" to creditors for three to five years. In recent years courts in different districts – sometimes within the same state – have seized on the inherent ambiguity in these standards to impose widely varying requirements for good faith proposals and measures of disposable income, creating a "local legal culture" among US bankruptcy courts (Kilborn 2005).

Chapter 13 offers individuals a number of advantages over liquidation under Chapter 7. Perhaps most significantly, Chapter 13 offers individuals an opportunity to save their homes from foreclosure. By filing under this chapter, individuals can stop foreclosure proceedings and may remedy delinquent mortgage payments over time. Nevertheless, they must still make all mortgage payments that become due during the Chapter 13 plan on time. Another advantage of Chapter 13 for the over-indebted is that it allows individuals to reschedule secured debts (other than a mortgage for their primary residence) and extend them over the life of the plan. Doing this may lower the payments. Chapter 13 also has a special provision that protects third parties who are liable with the debtor on "consumer debts". This provision may protect co-signers. Chapter 13 acts like a consolidation loan under which the individual makes the plan payments to a trustee who then distributes payments to creditors. Individuals will have no direct contact with creditors while under Chapter 13 protection.

The United Kingdom

In the UK bankruptcy is divided into separate local regimes for England and Wales, for Northern Ireland and for Scotland. There is also a UK insolvency law which applies across the UK. Notwithstanding that Scotland is part of the UK, it retains its own separate legal system. In Scotland, bankruptcy is called "sequestration", and the organization responsible for administering its processes is the Accountant in Bankruptcy. In the following we concentrate on the system applied in England and Wales.

The payment collection procedure in the UK follows a similar path to the US. Before issuing a claim, the creditor (claimant) must send the debtor (defendant) a detailed letter setting out a clear summary of the facts on which the claim is based, enclosing any supporting documents and giving the debtor a reasonable time to respond (Euler Hermes 2017). The debtor should answer confirming whether or not the claim is accepted. If the debtor disagrees, he or she should respond with evidence in support of that position. The court expects both parties to act reasonably in attempting to resolve matters before proceedings, and they should continue to act in this way throughout the claim. If that is not the case, the court has powers to penalize unreasonable behaviours.

In the UK, as elsewhere, legal action will usually be commenced when amicable collection has failed (Euler Hermes 2017). If the creditor goes to court, the claim will be issued by the court and served on the defendant, who is given 14 days from service to acknowledge the claim or file a defence. If the debtor acknowledges the claim within that timescale, he will be given a further 14 days (that is, a total of 28 days from service of the claim to file a defence); but if the debtor fails to file a defence to the claim, the creditor can apply to the court for default judgment. If the debtor does file a defence and the creditor considers that it is without merit and unlikely to succeed, the creditor can apply to the court for a strike out of the defence and/or summary judgment.

The court will usually list a hearing of the application and the creditor will need to show the court that the debtor has no reasonable prospect of defending the claim, and that there is no other reason why the claim should proceed to trial. If the claimant is successful, judgment will be entered against the debtor and the creditor can seek fixed costs of the application. If the debtor does file a defence to the claim, the court will allocate the claim to a particular track depending on its value.

Only after a judgment has been obtained, either by default or after trial, and if payment is not forthcoming from the judgment debtor, may the creditor take enforcement action. A judgment creditor may file an application to the court where judgment was obtained for a Warrant of Execution. This form of enforcement is used for smaller amounts of outstanding debt. A County Court Bailiff will attend the judgment debtor's address and request payment. The bailiff may levy upon goods to the equivalent value of the judgment debt. Unless invited, the bailiff will not be able to enter residential premises. A Warrant of Execution is initially for a 12-month period and may be extended upon application subsequently.

A judgment creditor may also make an application to the court for a Writ of Fieri Facias (Writ of Fi Fa). In simple terms this means that the court order gives an official the right to take a person's property in order to pay someone the money that person owes them. If the Writ of Fi Fa is warranted, the creditor can send it to a High Court Enforcement Officer (HCEO), also known as a Sheriff. The Sheriff will then seek to enforce the writ and add any fees, poundage or other costs of execution to the judgment debt. The Sheriff is able to levy upon goods to the equivalent value of the judgment debt to sell at auction to offset against the amount outstanding.

The third avenue for debt collection is charging orders which allow the judgment creditor to seek security over property owned by the judgment debtor (for example their home) to the value of the judgment debt. It is not strictly a "charge" over property but gives the judgment creditor an interest in the proceeds of sale of the property. Once a judgment creditor has a charging order they may be able to apply to the court for an order for sale of the property to which it relates. There should be available equity and the court will take a number of factors into account, such as whether the property is a family home.

In the UK, the term "bankruptcy" only applies to insolvent individuals; but these may have few or no assets such that the creditor may deem bankruptcy proceedings pointless because the unsecured creditor would receive a very low dividend or no dividend at all. Already the first Bankruptcy and Insolvency Act of 1883 was valid as the "poor man's bankruptcy" since it allowed an individual to repay a portion of debts and then write off any remaining balance after some years (Ramsay 2017, p. 1).

Bankruptcy proceedings in the UK are still used against individuals liable for undisputed debts over 750 British pounds, provided that the creditor is able to show that the debtor is unable to pay (Euler Hermes 2017). If a bankruptcy order is made, either the Official Receiver or a trustee in bankruptcy will attempt to realize assets for the benefit of creditors. There is no legislation on debt settlements, but Individual Voluntary Arrangements (IVA) may be concluded as a restructuration proceeding. The legally binding agreements between debtor and creditor normally last for five years, a period during which the debtor will be expected to pay into the IVA what he can afford outside reasonable living costs. All interest and charges will be frozen at 0 per cent, and creditors will be prohibited from demanding additional payments. Once an IVA is accepted by the creditor(s), an Insolvency Practitioner (IP) will monitor its progress.

The bankruptcy legislation in England and Wales – with swift discharge, straightforward access to the insolvency procedure and absence of any requirement to notify creditors before filing – has made the jurisdiction attractive also to "bankruptcy tourism" (Ramsay 2017, pp. 179–184). This means that individuals and companies from other countries file for bankruptcy in England or Wales.

Germany

Modern European debt collection systems, unlike the US system, eventually demand that the great majority of debtors make at least an attempt at repayment of debt. What is important for the debtor is that the obligation to use future income to pay debts will last several years (Kilborn 2005). As outlined above, Heuer (2013) identifies two approaches to consumer bankruptcy in Western Europe: the "Germanic" liability model emphasizing the debtor's responsibility for debt payment; and a "Franco-Scandinavian" mercy model focusing on the debtor's deservingness for debt relief. It was not until 1999 that the German legal apparatus began to offer personal insolvency proceedings for over-indebted consumers and homeowners. In the second half of the 2000s, each year around 100 000 individuals took advantage of the new opportunity to declare insolvency and seek debt discharge (Mertens 2017).

The German Civil Code (Bürgerliches Gesetzbuch, BGB) empowers creditors to issue a notice of cancellation of the credit agreement already after two instalments are overdue (Euler Hermes 2017). While the debtor may have had financial difficulties for an extended period ("hidden over-indebtedness"), it is the cancellation of the credit agreement that constitutes formally the status of over-indebtedness. This formal status signifies that the debtor is now in debt for the entire amount of outstanding credit(s), possibly leading to subsequent (wage) attachments (Haas 2006).

If the amicable phase fails or if the debtor questions the claim, the debtor can commence ordinary legal action (*Klageverfahren*) (Euler Hermes 2017). The court serves a summons to the debtor. The court schedules preliminary hearings (*früher erster Termin*) and written proceedings (*schriftliches Vorverfahren*) in order to consider the parties' arguments. The court would also attempt to set up a conciliation phase (*Güteverhandlung*) as part of these proceedings. When the debt is certain and undisputed, and provided that the debtor's assets are traceable, German creditors may rely on fast-track payment order procedures (*Mahnbescheid*) before the local court (*Amtsgericht*). This process forces the debtor to react within two weeks (that is, pay the debts or oppose the order). Any defence raised by the debtor, however, leads to resolving the dispute through a regular lawsuit. A main hearing would then take place to enable the court to render a judgment.

Enforcement may commence once a judgment is not appealed and is final (Euler Hermes 2017). Once the enforcement action is issued, a local bailiff attached to the district court will be instructed with enforcement of the writ and will proceed accordingly (auction of the debtor's assets, garnishment allowing payment from a third party and so on) upon payment of a fee. Court decisions also allow the closure of bank accounts or the seizure and sale of property (*Zwangsversteigerung*). The general prescription period (*Verjährungsfristen*) in Germany is three years, commencing at the end of the year in which the claim arises or in which the creditor obtains knowledge of the circumstances giving rise to the claim (subjective limitation period). That applies only to unpaid non-judgment debts. The statute of limitation for judgment debts can be as long as 30 years.

The German legislature (*Insolvenzordnung*) offers a complete discharge of unpaid debts, but it imposes weighty demands on consumer debtors, who must cede to creditors all of their non-exempt income for six years (rebates of portions of that income after the fourth and fifth years). However, the Civil Procedure Reforms of 2002 mandate that the creditors must enter into conciliation or mediation in order to reach a compromise as a prerequisite to formal judicial proceedings. As a result, most negotiations with German debtors terminate with an amicable settlement (which may include a payment instalment or a debt write-off) which is generally respected.

Due to the mandatory process of conciliation Germany has comprehensive information about debt counselling clients, as shown in Table 2.4. The figures from debt counselling for 2016 reveal that a clear majority of more than 600 000 annual cases concern households with very low net incomes, that is, below 1300 euros a month.

Table 2.4   Debt counselling clients and outstanding debt by monthly household net income in 2016, euros

	All	Below 900	900– 1300	1300– 1500	1500– 2000	2000– 2600	2600– 3600	3600 and above
Share	617 237	36.3%	23.8%	9.4%	15.7%	9.5%	4.4%	0.9%
Average debt, €	31 613	24 364	27 126	31 970	35 263	43 095	57 573	121 846

Source: Statistisches Bundesamt (2017).

Debt settlement proceedings in Germany are governed by the Insolvency Act (*Insolvenzordnung "InsO"*) amended in 2012. Following a petition filed before the Insolvency Court (*Insolvenzgericht*) on the basis of illiquidity, imminent illiquidity or over-indebtedness, the court may open preliminary insolvency proceedings. This process is only available to those default-debtors "with not too many debts and creditors" as the criterion is worded in the German law provisions. To initiate personal bankruptcy proceedings the debtor has to ask out of court all the creditors if they would agree on a payment plan with a monthly or other periodic payment of part of the outstanding debt. The purpose is to come to an "administration or voluntary arrangement under the Insolvency Act" with all creditors. The debtor needs to send a letter to all creditors explaining his financial situation and asking them to file their claim once more exactly and in detail; he must also mention all other creditors he has with their amount of claim. The debtor will propose a payment plan and set a deadline to declare whether the creditor agrees to this plan.

The debtor is legally entitled to propose to pay nothing to the creditors ("zero plan") if he or she has no earnings or assets. If a proposal of a payment plan fails and only one of the creditors objects/rejects the plan, the debtor has to file bankruptcy proceedings with the court. The debtor informs the court that he or she has tried to come to an agreement with all creditors according to legal obligations and according to the legal provisions in such proceedings. The debtor then applies to institute bankruptcy proceedings managed by the court. The application to the court must be very detailed; for example, debtors must disclose all the assets they have had in the past three years and explain what has happened to them. The court will suggest a new payment plan to all creditors. Bankruptcy proceedings often last several years. One reason for that is the fact that many default-debtors have a number of unpaid debts. Around 40 per cent of debtors have more than nine creditors (Table 2.5).

Table 2.5   *Number of creditors and balance of outstanding debt in Germany among debt counselling clients in 2016*

Number of creditors	1	2–4	5–9	10–19	20+
Share of all debtors	12.7%	20.7%	25.7%	26.1%	14.8%
Outstanding debt (€)	below 10 000	10 000– 25 000	25 000– 50 000	50 000– 100 000	100 000 and above
Share of all debtors	39.5%	28.5%	18.1%	8.2%	5.7%

Source: Statistisches Bundesamt (2017).

The German system emphasizes the concept of "fairness", since every debtor is called upon to make the same predictable sacrifice. The German system leaves very little discretion for local authorities to alter the balance of costs and benefits each debtor can expect (Kilborn 2005). In 2014, the debt settlement payment period was reduced to three years for those debtors who are able to pay a portion of their debts.

The Netherlands

As opposed to many other countries the creditor in the Netherlands is not obliged to warn the debtor of a decision to take legal action. However, the creditor normally commences legal dunning with a registered demand letter recalling the debtor's obligation to pay the principal, together with late payment (Euler Hermes 2017). Also in the Netherlands, the creditor can rely on a simplified fast-track alternative to ordinary legal proceedings, but this normally requires that the debt (below 25 000 euros) be certain and undisputed. Legal action will commence when the creditor serves the debtor with a summons through a bailiff, and the debtor would normally be given six weeks to file a defence. The limitation period of an invoice is five years, while the period is 20 years for judgment.

Bankruptcy proceedings would commence when the debtor has ceased paying and the district court declares the debtor bankrupt. Bankruptcy, if requested by a creditor, will only be declared if there are at least two creditors with overdue claims. If bankruptcy is declared at the debtor's own request, however, there is no need for the second creditor.

The court process for handling insolvent debtors in the Netherlands differs significantly from the other countries in this study, but it is clearly in favour of the creditor. The Dutch Bankruptcy Act 1893 (*Faillissementswet*) treats insolvency through different procedures, but liquidation tends to prevail. The term "debt restructuring" or "rescheduling" under insolvency law in the Netherlands traditionally applies restrictively to private individuals. The criterion for debt restructuring is that a plan would be approved by ⅔ of the creditors representing ¾ of the debt. There are no legal limits to the amounts to be written off. During debt restructuring, suspension of payments or bankruptcy proceedings, a moratorium is put into place from the moment the court has issued an adjudication order until the termination of the insolvency. As a result, creditors cannot enforce payment of their claims unless they hold exclusive rights (RoT, mortgage, right of distraint) (Euler Hermes 2017).

In 2008 the Netherlands adopted three new legal remedies for the Debt Adjustment Act (European Consumer Debt Network 2013). Firstly, the law compels those creditors to agree on debt settlement who unreasonably refuse to agree to an amicable settlement. Secondly, the court can decide on a six-month cooling-off period during which debtors can attempt an amicable settlement while creditors are temporarily unable to exercise their rights. Thirdly, the law established preliminary relief as an emergency measure for the period between submission of the application for debt management and a court decision in respect of the application.

An important feature of the consumer insolvency procedure in the Netherlands is that the outcome of a debt restructuring does not necessarily entail a debt discharge. Applications for discharge are only admissible if previous out-of-court negotiations have failed. When a debt restriction is granted, a period of good conduct is imposed, generally three years but possibly up to five years. During this period, the debtor is granted only an income comparable to the minimum wage from his or her work by the rescheduling administrator. In addition, the administrator directly receives and checks all of the debtor's mail during the first 13 months of the period of good conduct. According to Klein (2016), this "draconian regime" encourages Dutch households to slash consumption and prioritize debt repayment.

Finland

In Finland, a payment default entry is the result of extended payment difficulties (on average from six to eight months) and is recorded when neglect of payment has been confirmed by a court decision or by the execution authority (Euler Hermes 2017). Legal dunning is to start with a Demand Letter (registration is not necessary in Finland) recalling the debtor's obligation to pay the principal, together with late payment interest (as contractually agreed or taking a legal rate as a reference), within seven days. Undisputed claims in Finland would normally be solved within three to six months, but when the claims are disputed legal proceedings could take about a year.

The creditor would start ordinary legal action when amicable collection has failed (Euler Hermes 2017). He will leave a written application for summons with the registry of the district court, which then serves the debtor with a Writ of Summons. If the court determines that the debt is certain and undisputed, fast-track proceedings in the court would first request a simplified Payment Order (*suppea haastehakemus*) on the basis of any invoice, contract or debt recognition title available. The debtor is then given approximately two weeks to file a defence; failure to reply would tend to lead to a default judgment in favour of the claimant. Otherwise, the court will examine the parties' evidence and arguments before rendering a decision.

After a court decision imposing a liable payment, creditors can turn to the Finnish enforcement authority. Public debts to the state (for example penalty fees, taxes and insurance premiums) can be collected by enforcement without a separate court judgment (Oksanen et al. 2015). A judgment on civil and commercial claims is enforceable for 15 years as soon as it becomes final (that is, when all appeal venues have been exhausted), whereas in criminal cases debts are enforceable for 20 years. Debts to the state, for example taxes, are valid for five years.

If the debtor fails to abide by the judgment, the creditor will enforce it through a bailiff, who will try to obtain an instalment agreement with the debtor or enforce it through seizure of assets. As a general rule, one-third of the debtor's income is garnished. It is also possible to garnish tax refunds and capital income. A debtor in Finland is regarded as insolvent if he or she is permanently unable to pay his or her debts when they fall due. The debtor can seek refuge in filing an application for reorganization of an undertaking, which is also called debt settlement. It can be also initiated following a petition to the court by the creditors. This procedure is intended for those with larger debts and is not available for minor overdue payments which are enforced.

The law on debt settlement (*velkajärjestely*), which came into force in 1993, established the rules and regulations under which a settlement can be enforced by the court. The first criterion is a state of insolvency, that is, the default-debtor is permanently unable to repay his debts. However, the debtor also needs to have some regular income beyond the bare minimum to pay a portion of his or her overdue debts. This is a matter of calculation where all the applicant's income, expenses and assets are considered.

Once granted, a debt settlement implies that the default-debtor can keep an apportioned part of their income to cover basic needs, including housing costs (they may retain possession of their house) and reasonable special needs such as medicines. The rest is set aside to repay debts. The debt settlement lasts three years, but may be extended to five years if the debts are from consumption credits and if they are not related to unemployment or sickness. Mortgage debtors may keep their property if they are able to repay the mortgage without interest. In this case the debt settlement lasts ten years. Finnish legislation does not allow bankruptcy for private persons.

Norway

Payment default was not decriminalized in Norway until 1983. Since then Norwegian legislation has included the possibility of debt discharge. As in Finland, if the debt is certain and undisputed, a bailiff is first entitled to issue a Payment Order, which is given the same value as a court judgment (Euler Hermes 2017). Thus, if the debtor does not pay as requested, the bailiff may commence forced execution. If the debtor disputes the debt, however, the case must be solved through the Concili-ation Board (*forliksråd*) or through an ordinary lawsuit (Euler Hermes 2017). In Norway, most civil disputes are considered initially by the Conciliation Boards, which are to be found in every municipality and consist of lay people. The creditor would normally file a claim with the District Court, which would invite the parties to a meeting in order to identify their claims and organize hearings to collect evidence and arguments prior to rendering a decision.

In Norway, a judgment is enforceable for ten years provided that it has become final – that is, when all avenues of appeal have been exhausted (Euler Hermes 2017). If the debtor fails to satisfy the judgment, the

creditor may request compulsory enforcement by the enforcement authorities, who will then seize the debtor's assets and funds in order to pay the
claim.

Norwegian bankruptcy legislation includes private individuals but it is
not used by them. The Debt Settlement Act was introduced in 1993 as a
direct response to the effects of the debt crisis (Poppe et al. 2016). It
gives debtors the opportunity to be discharged of hopeless debt loads by
committing themselves to a thrifty life for a limited period of time –
normally five years (Poppe 2008, p. 20). It also prevents debtors from
losing their homes whenever it can be avoided. For creditors the Act
gives access to free-of-charge, transparent and fair process to coordinate
all claims from all involved claimants while also establishing a template
which encourages voluntary out-of-court proceedings.

As in Finland the main criterion for qualifying for debt settlement in
Norway is that the default-debtor is permanently unable to repay the
debts. The consideration takes into account the applicant's income,
expenses and assets, and weighs them against the outstanding claims.
When assessing the ability to pay the future prospects for improvements
with regard to the applicant's age, education, health and labour market
developments are also taken into account. Another criterion in Norway is
that a debt settlement must not be morally offensive to the general public
(Poppe 2008, p. 20). This criterion involves a number of circumstances
with regard to the proposed standards of living, the character of the debts
and the default-debtor's behaviour vis-à-vis the creditors. However, very
few applicants are excluded since the very purpose of the Act is to help
also those who have behaved irresponsibly in the past.

During a debt settlement, the default-debtors have the right to keep a
certain portion of their income, including means to cover reasonable
special needs such as medicines, medical treatment and visiting rights
with their own children (Poppe 2008, p. 20). If the debtors comply with
the debt settlement, all remaining debts are written off. However, that
does not concern mortgages if the agreement includes homeownership.

COMPARING PERSONAL INSOLVENCY REGIMES

In terms of debt collection before court proceeding, all the countries
apply fairly similar systems (for example Euler Hermes 2017). The
countries have tried to simplify the process by introducing fast-track
procedures or summary mechanisms for obvious cases of default. The
aim is to speed up the process to determine payment obligation. In all
countries, the majority of consumer cases are resolved without the debtor

raising a defence. The countries also offer a similar range of options, including forced sale of property, wage attachments and closure of bank accounts.

Table 2.6　Central features of debt discharge systems in six countries

Country	Immediate debt discharge possible?	Duration of debt settlement	How long is judgment debt enforceable?
US	Yes	Immediate	Depends on state, typically 3–6 years
UK	Yes	Immediate Chapter 13: 3–5 years	6 years
Germany	No	3–6 years	30 years
Netherlands	No	3–5 years	20 years
Finland	No	3–10 years	15 years
Norway	No	3 years	10 years

The modern Western European consumer bankruptcy systems in Finland, Germany, the Netherlands and Norway with no immediate debt discharge and longer duration of debt settlement differ substantially from the mature Anglo-Saxon systems in the US and the UK (Table 2.6). Furthermore, in the first category we may distinguish the German liability model and the Nordic mercy mode (Heuer 2013). The German model is based on an economic and moral view of consumer bankruptcy that excludes primarily NINA debtors by means of long payment periods, cost hurdles and educational/behavioural obligations. In the Nordic model the bankruptcy officials exclude debtors who do not seem "deserving enough" by means of access screenings, adjustable procedures and broad discretionary powers.

According to Heuer (2013) both European debt relief models can be questioned in terms of costs and efficiency and in terms of fairness and justice. From the debtors' perspective, the main problem is that both approaches exclude a significant share of insolvent individuals from relief. Heuer asserts that the debt settlement systems in Finland and Norway do not give the majority of debtors the opportunity for a fresh start. His argument is based on three claims: strict access screenings exclude debtors who are deemed "not needy enough"; adjustable procedures pose problems of unpredictability and unfairness, and result in high shares of abandoned cases; and broad discretionary powers for officials invite "moral conservatism", high numbers of access denials, highly demanding payment plans and vast regional variation.

The opportunity for a debt discharge is undeniably important in providing a fresh new start for over-indebted individuals. However, it does not give the full picture of the situation. As described above, not everyone can file for personal insolvency. The reasons could be structural (such as cost of the process, legal obstacles) or personal (for example effort not to lose a home or credit scores, collateral or surety given by a family member, relative or a friend). Additionally, the analysis above did not disclose the effects of debt settlements on access to future credit. Poor credit scores or payment default entries in public records may not only prevent people from having a credit card or mortgage but may also cause problems with getting a job or renting accommodation (CPEC 2013, p. 189; Poppe 2008, p. 46; Ford 1988, p. 137).

3.   Causes of over-indebtedness

Why did one of the most famous painters of all time get into serious financial problems and become forced to declare bankruptcy? Obviously Rembrandt was not as skilful in handling money as he was in handling colours (Crenshaw 2006). But was Rembrandt's bankruptcy in 1686 caused by a pattern of financial recklessness and other types of personal failure or by a change in external circumstances? Researchers have long debated the issue. In one of the first biographies of Rembrandt, published in 1686, Filippo Baldinucci attributed the bankruptcy to Rembrandt's eccentric character, expressed in excessive collecting of art and buying back his own prints to inflate their prices. Rembrandt had an insatiable desire for collecting art and antiquities (he paid the highest recorded price in his time for a single seashell), and spent lavishly on paraphernalia for his studio and *kunstkamer*. H. Perry Chapman (2006) stresses the importance of Rembrandt's decision to buy a house which was beyond his means. Paul Crenshaw's account emphasizes Rembrandt's "manner of evading his responsibility to his creditors". When in financial difficulty Rembrandt frequently failed to conform to his clients' expectations or meet their demands. In 1653 Rembrandt realized that he would not be able to repay his debts. To save his neck, he engaged in practices which were barely legal but socially disreputable (Crenshaw 2006, p. 2). More contemporary scholars have pointed to external circumstances in terms of an oversaturated art market and declining economy due to the First Anglo-Dutch War. This case will not be solved, but it illustrates the complexities surrounding causes of over-indebtedness.

It is obvious that poor people always struggle with paying bills and making ends meet. However, over-indebtedness is recognized as a social problem only when it concerns a larger share of the population. Capitalist economies have undergone tremendous transformations over the last centuries, but the mechanism leading to households' large-scale debt problems has remained unchanged. A marked reduction in the demand for labour, a typical sign of economic recession, is a direct and immediate causal mechanism linking structural changes with household debt problems. The economic crises hit hardest those who suffer unemployment, and among them especially those who are tempted to buy properties when the markets were overheated before the recession. The scissor movement of reduced incomes and higher costs of loans leads to tremendous human suffering in terms of foreclosures and evictions.

Before the 20th century institutionalized borrowing was mostly the privilege of the wealthy (Ford 1988). Those with money were able to borrow more; those with no money found it difficult to borrow at all. Borrowing became more institutionalized in the US and Europe in the early 1900s. With the rise of instalment selling households set out slowly on the path to indebtedness (Caplovitz 1967; Ford 1988; Mian and Sufi 2015a). With an overhaul of usury laws and the selling of consumer goods with credit consumer debts became economically and socially acceptable in the US already in the first quarter of the 1900s. In Europe, that did not happen until the end of the Second World War.

With regulated credit markets during the decades after the Second World War the capitalist economies experienced a historical period of security and prosperity. This period coincided with the construction of more or less developed welfare states in all Western countries (Esping-Andersen 1990; Korpi and Palme 1998). Social engineers, such as William Beveridge in the UK and Gunnar and Alva Myrdal in Sweden, who designed comprehensive welfare state policies after the Second World War did not consider over-indebtedness as a social risk which would necessitate intensive attention. This was perhaps because the risk of over-indebtedness did not touch upon the growing masses of the middle class. The income replacement programmes for the old, sick and unemployed helped prevent over-indebtedness and supported those over-indebted hurt by these risks. The situation changed when large-scale economic crises, starting with the oil crises in 1973, hit world markets. Global economic crises starting in 2008 took the heaviest toll in terms of over-indebtedness.

Each country has its own narrative of economic and debt crises as well as trajectories of household over-indebtedness. In the following, we will review the different experiences of recessions preceding the Global economic crisis in Western countries, with a special emphasis on the six countries specifically discussed in this book. We first discuss development in the US and UK, then focus on Germany and the Netherlands, and finally analyse the Nordic context. The discussion is followed by an analysis of the context of Global economic crises. Then we will present a conceptual framework to analyse the causes of over-indebtedness in detail, and later use this framework to discuss the particular causes mentioned.

LIBERALIZATION OF CONSUMER CREDIT MARKETS

As a leading capitalist economy, the US gave an example for European financial markets to use credit to finance private consumption. Since the early 1900s consumer credit has been an important instrument in realizing the American dream. Living on credit has allowed consumers to achieve lifestyles commensurate with better days that surely lay ahead (Kilborn 2005). The decades preceding the Global economic crises witnessed the expansion of household debt burdens in the US. For example, between 1989 and 2006, total consumer credit card debt quadrupled. This development was fuelled by credit industry deregulation, including key legislative decisions in 1978 and 1996. With its 1978 decision in *Marquette National Bank of Minneapolis v. First of Omaha Service Corp* the US Supreme Court all but abolished effective regulation of consumer lending, which accelerated the explosion of consumer credit. The unanimous decision held that state anti-usury laws regulating interest rates cannot be enforced against nationally chartered banks based in other states. According to Kilborn (2005) the consumers were left largely to their own devices in choosing whether and to what extent to take on debt. In the run-up to the financial collapse of 2008 the subprime lending industry targeted those low-income households which still had been outside the mortgage and homeownership market, specifically Hispanic and African American communities.

Before the Great Recession in 2008, debt levels rose in all Western countries. In the UK, the time of the happy middle class ended in the 1980s. Unemployment climbed to permanently higher levels. The liberal economic policy introduced by Margaret Thatcher in the 1980s encouraged low-income households to own their own homes as part of the government's political ideology. The policy was promoted with cutbacks in the quantity and quality of local authority rentals, rising rents and long waiting lists for public housing (Ford 1988, p. 87). The relaxation of controls over building societies in 1986 improved access to credit. The "Right to Buy" scheme pushed local authorities to unroll their ownership of rentals by selling them to the tenants (Poppe 2008, p. 40). The prices were low, but poor households still needed to borrow money to make the purchase. Homeownership became an achievement and a sign of social success. But the optimism faded when unemployment started to increase. Thatcher's labour market reforms created a large, secondary labour market characterized by temporary or part-time work contracts and low wages at the expense of full-time employment. The precarious labour market conditions led to mounting economic difficulties, and home-ownership became unsustainable.

An important part of Thatcher's neoliberal policy package was de-regulation of credit markets. There is obviously a positive, macro-level correlation between post-deregulation credit volumes and the spread of over-indebtedness (Huls et al. 1994). Deregulation denotes increase in the number of market actors, in new products and in the volume of marketing, which may simply provide some households with too much credit. During the regulation period households may not have had experience of the consequences of market fluctuations to household economy. At the time of the issue a debt load may seem reasonable, but structural and individual changes in the debt/income ratio make them vulnerable to debt problems. Increase in credit volume also comes from households which previously had no access to credit due to limited economical means, including young people. They have higher risks of default.

Deregulation of credit markets in the late 1970s and 1980s created hugely profitable new consumer credit markets. Consumer finance was a booming area of money making. That led to substantial increases in consumer debt and mortgages. In the UK, the household debt-to-income level increased from 90 per cent in 1987 to 160 per cent in 2007 (Bunn and Rostom 2015).

The UK, among other countries, experienced a housing price bubble at the turn of the 1990s. Economic downturn hit the UK in the early 1990s. The deflationary pressures caused by high real and nominal interest rates and currency overvaluation ended when the UK was forced to abandon the policy of exchange rate targeting in the autumn of 1992 and let its currency float. Higher interest rates pushed up the loan servicing burden, followed by arrears and repossessions of newly acquired houses. Eviction or foreclosure came not only with instability but also with loss. Besides their possessions, families lost their only home, school, neighbourhood.

In Germany consumer credit volumes increased tenfold between 1970 and 1991; if mortgages are included, the volume doubled from 1987 to 1997. However, the situation changed completely in the 2000s. While credit volumes expanded in other countries, bank loans to households declined dramatically in volume as a percentage of GDP (Mertens 2017). Despite this development Mertens argues that credit has continued to gain importance for social security in Germany through promotion of personal saving schemes, private households' compensatory borrowing and expansion of quasi-public financial institutions with targeted loan programmes.

Housing policy favouring homeownership has dramatically increased household debt levels in the Netherlands (OCED 2017a). Household debt increased in the Netherlands between 2000 and 2007 even more than in the US (Mian and Sufi 2015a, p. 6). In 2014, as many as 1.5 million households held negative housing equity in the Netherlands (Klein 2016). The high number is attributed to the fact that the consumer insolvency procedure is not so attractive for holders of negative housing equity because debt discharge may not be granted.

Until the mid-1980s the credit markets were tightly regulated in Finland and Norway. Due to slow urbanization there was not a huge demand for loans either. Loans became common only in the 1960s, when people moved to cities and bought flats (Raijas et al. 2010). In those days, households faced tight liquidity constraints. They were not allowed to borrow as much as they would have liked; only long-standing and most trustworthy bank customers were granted mortgages. Hardly anybody defaulted, and if somebody did it was attributed to personal faults.

In Norway, legislation passed in the early 1980s permitted independent housing cooperatives to dissolve and sell properties at market prices since the maximum prices on flats belonging to public building projects were removed at the same time (Poppe 2008, p. 40). The total credit volume among households in Norway increased nearly threefold from 153 billion to 450 billion kroner between 1981 and 1988 (Poppe 2008, p. 49).

The housing markets and the credit markets were also deregulated in Finland towards the end of the 1980s with the introduction of free capital movement and the end of credit rationing and controlled interest rates. Foreign capital fuelled the credit expansion. As a result, consumption, investments and asset prices soared. Deregulated housing and credit markets raised the proportion of homeowners but also increased debt loads of households. Having almost unlimited access to credit made some private individuals also use loans to buy stocks and make other types of high-risk investments. Relying on earlier experience, debtors did not expect debt servicing to cause problems because earnings were growing rapidly and the real after-tax interest rate was expected to remain low due to modest levels of nominal interest and tax deductions (Kiander and Vartia 2011).

Following the New York stock exchange collapse in October 1987, the housing market began to collapse in Norway. This became known as the "debt crisis", which lasted nearly six years. It was not until 1997 that housing prices returned to previous levels. Previously very rare forced sales became commonplace. Even middle-class families risked losing their homes. In the peak year of 1990 there were more than 22 000 forced sales (Poppe 2008, p. 15).

While Norway went into recession in the late 1980s the economy of Finland continued to overheat. The boom did not end until 1990 when international interest rates started to increase. The Finnish economy relied heavily on barter trade with the Soviet Union. When the Soviet Union dissolved, the Finnish economy went down like a stone. Between 1991 and 1993, GDP dropped by 12 per cent and the unemployment rate rose from 3.5 to 18 per cent (Kalela et al. 2001). The crisis, as estimated by production losses, was even deeper than during the Great Depression of the 1930s. Economists include the crises of Norway in 1987 and Finland in 1991 among the big five post-war banking crises in the developed countries (Mian and Sufi 2015a, p. 7).

The economic crisis had the greatest impact on those who lost their job, their company, their property and/or their credit rating or who had guarantee liabilities (Kiander and Vartia 2011). Many small businesses went bankrupt and left their previous owners with immense debts. Also, people who had to sell their housing property due to unemployment and/or skyrocketing mortgage rates were left with large debts when housing prices went down (Blomgren et al. 2016). In many cases they ended up in a situation where their mortgages exceeded the value of their house (negative asset value). The effects of the debt crises were aggravated by the fact that loan-making routines with regard to collateral and personal guarantees during credit expansion followed the practice adopted at the time when credit availability was strictly regulated. The banks, for example, demanded personal guarantees not only for business loans but also for mortgages and other types of consumer loans. Sometimes personal guarantees were obtained from relatives and friends, who were naive enough to comply since similar commitments had previously been completely risk-free.

The number of over-indebted persons grew steeply during the early 1990s in Finland. In 1994, as many as 457 000 persons from a population of about 5.1 million were subject to debt enforcement activities (Muttilainen 2002). In the same year, 313 000 persons had a payment default entry in the credit information register, meaning that payment had been in arrears for on average six to eight months (Rantala and Tarkkala 2009). Kiander and Vartia (2011) argue that the main causes of the exceptionally deep recession in Finland were the deregulation of the financial markets in the 1980s and the subsequent overheating, during which asset prices and debts doubled. The consequences of the bursting of this financial bubble were currency and banking crises, large fiscal deficits, mass unemployment, collapsing asset prices and widespread over-indebtedness.

GLOBAL ECONOMIC CRISIS

Throughout the 2000s, household debt relative to disposable income rose in most OECD countries (European Commission 2008a). With expansion of credit and overly optimistic expectations about future economic and housing price developments, including low interest rates, mortgage lending soared in most OECD countries in the run-up to the Global economic crisis which shook the world economy beginning in 2008 (André 2016). In particular, the Global economic crisis, preceded by easy access to credit, revealed the hidden epidemic of over-indebtedness.

André identifies two categories of OECD countries with the steepest rises in mortgage delinquencies following the crisis. In the first category mortgage defaults were mostly attributed to excessive risk taking in mortgage lending, although deteriorating economic conditions also played a role. The outstanding example is the US subprime crisis. Several subprime borrowers were only able to repay as housing prices increased. When prices stopped rising, defaults and foreclosures skyrocketed. The second category consists of countries where falling income and rising unemployment during the downturn caused defaults on mortgages. In these cases, common in European countries, most of the increase in delinquencies followed the deterioration in economic conditions.

The Global economic crisis resulted in the loss of 8 million jobs between 2007 and 2009 in the US. More than 4 million homes were lost to foreclosures (Mian and Sufi 2015a, p. 2). Between 2006 and 2011 home values fell by 26 per cent in the US overall, and by more than 50 per cent in some states. At the end of 2011 as many as 15 per cent of homeowners had negative home equity and another 7.5 per cent had only minimal home equity (less than 10 per cent of home value) (Meltzer et al. 2013). Low-income Hispanic and African American communities were hit the hardest. Between 2007 and 2010 average white families lost 11 per cent of their wealth, while the corresponding figure for black families was 31 per cent and for Hispanic households 44 per cent (Desmond 2016, p. 125). Also Mian and Sufi (2015b) show that the credit bubble as well as ensuing over-indebtedness concerned especially those who had previous debt problems before entering the mortgage markets.

The importance of home equity-based borrowing in the US was reflected in the fact that the increase in debt was especially large among individuals in the lowest 60 per cent of the credit score distribution living in high house price growth zip codes. The bottom 40 per cent of the credit score distribution was responsible for 68 per cent of the total delinquencies in 2008, while individuals in the top 40 per cent of the initial credit score distribution did not make up more than 15 per cent of total delinquencies, even in 2009 at the height of the default crisis (Mian and Sufi 2015b).

During the years before 2008, most EU citizens were able to take on more debt than ever, and because of the positive future forecasts they also relied on their ability to pay it back. However, because of unemployment, decreasing wage rates, melting financial investments and reduced social benefits they have faced problems surviving with their debts. In the UK, the number of mortgage repossessions rose sharply as the economic downturn took effect after the economic collapse of 2008. The weak points of the UK regulatory framework for mortgage lending came to light when the crisis hit the US with serious repercussions for the UK. As it became apparent, many consumers had been able to obtain mortgages of a value well exceeding their underlying assets – their homes. Mortgages were also granted without verification of income. Empirical studies indicate that prior to the crisis, when the housing market was at its peak, this was the case in over half of all mortgages (Financial Services Authority 2012). When housing prices collapsed, many borrowers got into financial difficulties. The number of mortgage repossessions almost doubled from 25 900 in 2007 to 47 700 in 2009. In 2010, however, the situation stabilized due to the fact that the government and the banks helped borrowers through loan restructuring or allowing them to postpone repayment (Fondeville et al. 2010).

A study conducted by the European Central Bank (ECB) demonstrated that during the crises in the euro area the percentage of households plagued by over-indebtedness increased by more than 10 per cent as a result of unemployment shock – defined as a 5 per cent probability of an employee losing their job (Caju et al. 2016). The study observed, interestingly, that countries with fewer over-indebted households before the shocks seem to be impacted the most severely by unemployment shocks.

Germany was among the economies hit the hardest by the Global economic crises due to its strong dependence on exports. However, Germany emerged from the crisis quickly, and stronger than almost any other country. This success story has been explained as the hard-won reward for strict economic management, combining fiscal conservatism and structural reforms of welfare and the labour market. Progressive narrative emphasizes the non-neoliberal dimensions of Germany's economic model including a Keynesian crisis response (Storm and Naastepad 2014). Germany was not completely spared from the eruptions in the financial market. The government had to rescue one bank, Hypo Real Estate.

The Dutch mortgage market was characterized by a high ratio of household debt to gross disposable income even before the crises. A generous tax deduction for interest on mortgage loans (*hypotheekrenteaftrek*) and a government guarantee scheme for low-income borrowers (Nationale Hypotheek Garantie) have incentivized Dutch households to take on large mortgages. Other contributing factors were the extensive social benefits system, the low unemployment rate, the good debt ethic, the relatively modest use of variable interest and the stable housing market (Mak 2015). Default rates were low. Cases with payment arrears were solved most often through temporary freezes on interest or relaxing the terms of repayment. The banks had a large number of underwater mortgages, meaning that the value of the underlying property was lower than the amount of the loan for which the security had been given. These homeowners tried to keep their house off the market in any event, which made them vulnerable to negative changes, for example a decrease in income or a divorce, which in some cases forced them to sell the house below the value of the mortgage.

Following the Global economic crisis two banks in the Netherlands, Landsbanki/Icesave and DSB Bank, went into bankruptcy. Two of the country's largest financial institutions (ING and SNS REAAL) received government support, and the Dutch government nationalized parts of Fortis Bank and ABN Amro. Assessment of Dutch consumers' financial situation showed that at the formal start of the crisis in 2008 households had enough of a financial buffer. The full impact of the crisis crept in during the following years. In 2013, the contribution of long-term loans to total household debt was still above 92 per cent (OECD 2013).

Households' financial situation in the Netherlands did not start to improve until 2015 (Jansen et al. 2015). The Dutch, however, remained as most indebted households in the euro area. Outstanding residential mortgage debt was worth twice the total disposable income earned by households at the end of 2015. Fittingly for a country where much of the population lives below sea level, about 30 per cent of Dutch homeowners had negative equity.

What is important with regard to household debt problems in the Nordic countries is that interest rates were kept low. The Nordics had learned their lesson from the 1990s. Norway came quickly out of the

Global economic crisis of 2008. In fact, Norway experienced more than 20 consecutive years of economic growth marked by rising incomes, growing property prices and marginal, even declining, levels of unemployment (Poppe et al. 2016). As a result of tight regulation Norwegian banks were only lightly affected by the Global economic crisis. Instead, the crisis has fuelled borrowing through falling interest rates and stable economic conditions. This time the crisis did not lead to banking crises in Finland either, despite the fact that stock prices plummeted and household debt loads increased. The Finnish banks had been cautious in issuing mortgages and consumer loans. Global economic crisis did not result in an abrupt surge in over-indebtedness. After initial rebound the Finnish economy remained stagnant until 2017. In July 2017 the number of people with a payment default entry in the credit information register was a record almost 373 000 (Suomen Asiakastieto 2017), while there were 449 512 debtors in enforcement (Findikaattori 2017).

Zinman (2015) argues that a key factor in explaining the growth in household debt in the 2000s relates to technological change in financial markets. The innovations in loan production included reductions in distribution costs, risk-based pricing, monitoring and repossession, and securitization and other secondary market innovations. Creditors excelled also in consumer persuasion through direct marketing, shrouded and teaser pricing, credit card introductory rates and penalty fees, and adjustable-rate mortgages. The germane reason behind mortgage growth is also that housing prices have increased, actually in some places skyrocketed. Income inequality can also increase debt through excess supply of credit (the rich loan money to the poor) and/or through boosting demand for credit (the poor borrow money from the rich to come closer to their standard of living).

CONCEPTUAL FRAMEWORK

The general mechanism operating in over-indebtedness is delusively simple. David Caplovitz (1967, pp. 105–115), who studied over-indebtedness in the city of New York, argued that it follows from the simple model that any explanation of the spread and distribution of debt problems becomes a quest for mechanisms that may alter the value of the debt/income ratio. Increase in the cost of debts can occur through accumulation of debt or through current debts getting more expensive. Over-indebtedness is caused by increase in the cost of debts, decrease in income or increase in the cost of living. These mechanisms will be explored in the following.

The equation has only two variables, the costs of servicing debts and incomes to cover these costs. Every consumer has to calculate these two variables to remain solvent. Both variables are conditioned by structural and individual factors which are deeply embedded in the temporal and societal context. The calculation is delusive for the fact that the concept of income is delusive. It is also important to note that the equation leaves out the costs of living. When it comes to factors propelling over-indebtedness we are not interested in the total amount of disposable income but in the portion of the income which is disposable for honouring debts. It is not reasonable to think that even the most overstretched household would spend all its money on paying back debts. Since all individuals and households need to spend a certain amount of money to cover basic needs such as food, clothes, shelter and health care, the money available for debts is also conditioned by the scope and the cost of these basic necessities.

It is reasonable to believe that over-indebtedness is a result of a combination of causes arising both from structural and individual factors. Causes of over-indebtedness can be traced by focusing on costs of debts, incomes and the cost of living (Table 3.1). The obvious structural causes increasing the cost of debts are linked to economic fluctuations and financial industry practices in making loans. With regard to cost of debts the individual causes relate to financial literacy (or the lack of it) and reckless lending behaviour. When it comes to the denominator, welfare state and labour markets play a dominant role as structural factors, while individual social risks (unemployment, sickness and so on) feature as important individual causes. For example, a high income-replacement rate unemployment insurance over a long period will limit the risk of default associated with job loss.

Table 3.1 Structural and individual factors for over-indebtedness by debt/income ratio

	Structural	Individual
Increase in the cost of debts	Economic fluctuations Financial industry	Financial illiteracy Business bankruptcy Reckless spending Bad luck
Decrease in income	Welfare state programmes Wage labour markets	Individual social risks with bearing on incomes
Increase in the cost of living	Utility costs (electricity, water, gas, telecommunications, etc.) Housing costs Childcare and child-related costs Education costs Health care costs Insurance and other financial services Other costs of living (food, transport, etc.)	Individual social risks with bearing on expenditure Unfortunate circumstances

INCREASE IN THE COSTS OF DEBTS: STRUCTURAL FACTORS

According to Mason and Jayadev (2014), the evolution of debt/income ratios over time depends on income growth, inflation and interest rates, independent of any changes in borrowing. Interest rates are nationally regulated but tend to converge in the global financial markets (Arghyrou et al. 2009). The direct cost of debt is the interest payment on borrowed capital. The costs of servicing debts are also determined by other terms of loan contracts. The difference between structural and individual factors affecting the cost of debts is elusive. Some of the items discussed under structural factors are also related to individual factors, and vice versa.

Economic Fluctuations

The most important factor affecting costs of loans relates to economic contractions, which largely remain a mystery for economists (Mian and Sufi 2015a, p. 2). Whatever the reason behind the economic crises, the effects are transmitted to individuals and households through reductions in incomes, most pronouncedly through unemployment, and higher relative or absolute costs of debts. The reduction of demand, most notably in domestic consumer markets, forces both smaller and bigger businesses to close shop and file for bankruptcy.

Fluctuations in economic activity are as old as the history of economics. What is perhaps new is that the emergence of paid labour among the middle class in the 20th century made it possible for large portions of the population to become homeowners, in many cases with sizeable mortgages. Public policies were also designed to accelerate homeownership, for example through tax credits and allowances for mortgages, expressing an ideology where owning one's home is a natural state, superior to renting in social, economic and physical terms. It provides potential for asset accumulation, transmission of wealth to the next generation and offers personal control over the quality, development and disposal of one's home (Ford 1988, p. 86).

In addition, many countries downgraded or suspended public programmes for rental housing at the beginning of the 1980s. Before deregulation housing markets also included public instruments such as building societies, state banks and housing cooperatives and welfare programmes, which kept part of the housing market beyond the reach of for-profit actors. During the expansionary phase of a business cycle, often fuelled by financial liberalization, financial institutions' lending standards are gradually relaxed, which leads to lending booms. They end up in banking crises, recession, reinvigorated regulation, and then again to new rounds of expansion, loosening regulations and debt problems.

Central banks, with their iron-clad task of preserving the value of money, try to enforce price stability through controlling the economy's money supply. The key tool for that purpose is to change the so-called discount interest rate, which is the rate at which banks can borrow money from the central bank. Consumer loans are not directly tied to the discount interest rate but are affected by it. In an effort to prevent overheating of the economy, central banks may try to raise interest rates. That will not only eventually increase individual debtors' interest payments but will also drive down the value of assets, including private property and stocks. In turn, that will also decrease the value of collateral, which may cause problems for some debtors.

At times of crisis, central banks may also modify interest rates to defend the value of a currency against pressure for devaluation. Devaluation of a country's currency has a tendency to increase prices as imported goods and services become more expensive. As explained above, central bank decisions will inflict pain on debtors. That may, however, be necessary to prevent uncontrollable collapse of the markets, with ensuing unemployment, foreclosures and all other calamities of a deep economic recession, or devaluation of the country's currency and ensuing inflation. Conversely, in a stagnating economy central banks will speed up recovery by lowering interest rates. That will ease the situation of over-indebted individuals but may increase risk for over-indebtedness since low interest rates may encourage people to take out loans they may not be able to repay.

Economic contractions are often accompanied by a decline in asset prices. As Mian and Sufi (2015a, p. 18) point out, the fundamental feature of debt is that the borrower is the one who bears the first losses of equity in the asset process. For example, if the value of a house with a 150 000 euros mortgage and 50 000 euros of equity drops by 25 per cent, the homeowner has lost his or her full investment. The cost of the loan in relation to equity will increase correspondingly. Instead of helping to share the risk of homeownership, a mortgage concentrates the risk on the most vulnerable party. Therefore, Mian and Sufi (2015a, pp. 29–30) call this debt "anti-insurance". This has grave consequences both for the concerned homeowner and the whole economy, as will be demonstrated in the following chapter.

Financial Industry

Deregulation has made diffusion of financial product innovations easier. All Western countries allow a multitude of financing options, from respectable to predatory and illegal. Companies marketing different lines of credit utilize sophisticated persuasion techniques. They are especially effective when combined with uncontrolled credit market liberalization. Finland relaxed credit regulation towards the end of 1980s, overheating the economy (Kiander and Vartia 2011). Consumers were used to tight credit regulations. They were easily persuaded by aggressive lenders to utilize almost every opportunity to get more credit, including in foreign currency, when restrictions were removed. When the bubble burst and the Finnish currency was devalued by more than 20 per cent, a large number of debtors defaulted (Muttilainen 2002).

One factor behind growing credit volumes is indeed the development of numerous financial products whereby one may pay for consumption through borrowing (Poppe 2008, p. 40). Advanced risk-assessing technologies and market segregation strategies with fine-tuned algorithms based on machine learning have enabled flexible and tailored credit products. Loan offers and credit card opportunities may lead to increasing debt burdens and more vulnerable risk profiles. They also manifest a normative acceptance for using credit as way to finance lifestyle needs and homeownerships to bridge the imbalance between income cycles and life cycles. It is also important to note that credit card debts are some of the most expensive forms of credit in the market. In the late 1990s the fastest growing group of credit card customers in the US was observed among those with incomes below the poverty line (Sullivan et al. 2000, pp. 23–24). The data between 1981 and 1997 showed a significant increase in credit card debts among bankrupts (Sullivan et al. 2000, pp. 108–140). A Norwegian study demonstrated a similar growth in consumer debts among those who applied for a debt settlement between 1999 and 2004 (Poppe and Tufte 2005).

The ultimate point of deregulation was reached in the US pre-crises years, when reckless financial industry practices if not caused, then surely contributed to, the great Global economic crisis. Mian and Sufi (2015a, p. 98, 102) find convincing evidence that new financial innovations of this time were basically bankers' vehicles to fool investors into buying very risky securities that were passed off as safe. This notion relates especially to mortgages which were packaged into securitized pools. Securitization of mortgages did not incentivize banks to screen and monitor borrowers, and it also prevented debt adjustments for those borrowers who had got into difficulties.

Some scholars have tried to exonerate the financial industry as a culprit by arguing that credit played only a passive role in the housing boom and bust of 2000 to 2010 (Foote et al. 2012; Adelino et al. 2016). This view ignores that fact that financial sector activities during the boom, such as incentives in securitization or fraudulent underwriting of mortgages, played a major role in the crises (Mian and Sufi 2015a). The securitization of subprime loans in the US was accompanied by the creation of opaque financing chains involving structured financial products. The market actors were not able to value these products, which created enormous uncertainty in the markets when it became obvious that defaults on subprime loans were set to increase dramatically.

In addition, the underwriting and securitization process in the US was plagued by asymmetries of information as well as by conflicts of interest (Mian and Sufi 2015a). Credit rating companies received fees from the issuers of the securities they rated. They were inclined to underestimate risks. Hardly anybody cared, though, since risks could be transferred to other investors. Lending standards were relaxed when compensation structures within financial institutions encouraged excessive risk taking and short-termism. Easy access to credit fuelled the housing bubble in the US. The opacity of financial structures and risks contributed to the international spillover of the subprime crisis. The crisis resulted in increasing debt problems, although with large differences across countries.

Martin Luther King Jr once noted that "every condition exits simply because someone profits from its existence" (Desmond 2016, p. 305). According to economic theory, there is a positive relationship between risk and expected yield. The greater the uncertainty of repayment, the higher is the creditor price for borrowing the money. Low-income households have no access to high-street markets, and they have to rely on expensive sources of credit, including mail order, payday loans, other licensed and unlicensed moneylenders, and pawnbrokers. These lines of credit come typically with frequent payment schedules, which may consume a large share of low-income households' disposable incomes. Already Caplovitz (1967, 1974), who interviewed poor households in New York in the 1960s, observed the "poverty penalty" – that is, the poor end up paying more for credit than those better off. Caplovitz's findings were later reflected in the US, where interest rates were considerably higher in the so-called high-risk or subprime markets. That was also the case with additional charges such as credit insurance.

In *Making Ends Meet* Caplovitz (1979) described how recession with high unemployment rates and inflation causing escalating expenditures puts particularly poor and blue-collar households into financial difficulties, and how they fall victim to predatory lenders. The obvious reason is the unequal distribution of resources along traditional class divides. Caplovitz argues that creditor misbehaviour and predatory lending practices are often part of the processes leading to over-extension, that is, when a household simply cannot make ends meet. In these cases, the debtors may not have access to more respectable lenders or they lack financial literacy to exhaust such options.

The financial industry's attempt to capture the low-income segment of the market has been facilitated through new risk-assessing technologies which are widely used to sell capital-intensive goods to social groups that were previously excluded from credit-based purchases (Sullivan et al. 2000; Soederberg 2014; Poppe et al. 2016). The technologies may be new but the practices are old. In his first book, Caplovitz (1967) described the vicious practices of door-to-door salesmen and phone scams. As one of the most outraged examples, Caplovitz recounts an incident In New York City, where a group of chiropractors phoned low-income residents informing them about free medical examinations. In every case they "revealed" health problems for which the practitioner offered costly treatments for which the patients were cajoled to sign instalment contracts.

In the low-income segment interest rates are high and maturities short. The credit is used by people facing financial strain to help them make ends meet. With charges the price of credit runs into several hundred converted to an annual rate of return. These credits are available not only in the US but throughout Europe as well. In the CPEC (2013, p. 153) study stakeholders in several EU Member States (including Finland and the UK) reported a rise in the use of high-cost short-term credit in the form of SMS loans, payday loans or unregulated lending. SMS loans were recognized as the most prevalent type, even in countries where there was an interest rate cap. The cap can be circumvented, for example, through "administrative fees".

Zinman (2015) reports that in the small-dollar loan markets that serve subprime and often low-income consumers, payday loan borrowers in 2010 spent 7.4 billion US dollars to borrow 40 billion dollars on maturities of mostly two to four weeks. This gives triple-digit annual rates of return. A typical payday loan amounts to a few hundred dollars in the US. In over 80 per cent of cases the loans are rolled over or followed by another loan within 14 days (Zinman 2015). The use of SMS loans accounted for a large increase in the number of court judgments for non-payment of credit between 2005 and 2008 in Finland (Valkama and Muttilainen 2008). Research in the UK showed a more than sixfold increase in the number of debt advice clients that had payday loans between January 2009 and December 2011 (CPEC 2013, p. 153).

In the CPEC (2013, p. 150) interviews almost 9 in 10 stakeholders reported that specific types of consumer credit, most often high interest rate credit from regulated lenders, were among the most important causes of household over-indebtedness in their country. A stakeholder from the UK noted:

> These companies are providing astronomical [interest] rates while just giving people money for a short time. In practice, we find people, the same ones, using these companies again and again and it is not just until the end of the month. The challenge for policy makers is to not completely kill the market for short-term lending – there might be important instances to cover short-term need, for example someone might need an expensive repair of their car which they need to go to work, so they need a loan until the end of the month. The problem is that these loans are in many cases helping people to sustain their debt beyond sustainability. (CPEC 2013, p. 154).

Low-income borrowers also pay huge amounts in bank account overdraft fees (Soederberg 2014). Both payday loans and bank overdrafts are only available for those with a checking (current) account. Other small-dollar products such as pawn shops, rent-to-own contracts and auto title loan markets (the borrower obtains a loan secured by a free-and-clear auto title) have also grown rapidly in the US. Borrowers with bad credit reports may also turn to illegal moneylenders, also called loan sharks.

The evidence on price dispersion of credit bears witness to the fact that the lenders enjoy over-power in the markets. Deregulation of the consumer credit market has introduced a frenzy of competition among purveyors of new, highly profitable products. Kilborn (2005) asserts that intense competitive pressures force lenders to advertise and structure their products in a manner that would take advantage (consciously or unconsciously) of powerful competitive forces – the psychological biases and weaknesses of their customers.

Representatives of the financial industry in the US have claimed that missing rungs in the lending ladder are a result of state regulations that outlaw the very products that would fill the gaps (Zinman 2015). However, the evidence suggests that state laws restricting high-cost consumer loans from non-bank providers, such as payday lenders, seem to alleviate the problem of high-interest credit. Zinman (2015) points to household choice inefficiencies in borrowing. There is a low penetration and low quality of the advice market for household liabilities. Zinman asks why third parties do not help households make better choices and share in the savings.

Deregulation and targeting of low-income consumers with extractive credit products development has been welcomed by business interests and households alike, since it is alleged to allow more consumption and adds to national prosperity as well as to business profits. Meanwhile there is no doubt that it also creates new routes to over-indebtedness. Unsecured, high-interest payday loans offered to families with unpaid debt or poor credit history have demonstrated that there is a business model at the bottom of every market. Consumer credit markets host extractive practices to the extent that the financial industry can be considered as a vector of a debt epidemic, similarly with the tobacco industry as a vector of a tobacco epidemic.

INCREASE IN THE COSTS OF DEBTS: INDIVIDUAL FACTORS

Describing individual routes to over-indebtedness, we may cite Leo Tolstoy's novel *Anna Karenina,* which starts with the famous sentence: "Happy families are all alike; every unhappy family is unhappy in its own way." The so-called Anna Karenina principle, according to which complex processes can get out of balance in many different ways, aptly characterizes default-debtors' careers. In the popular discourse, over-indebtedness is easily associated with reckless behaviour, sometimes called "financial imprudence", which ends up spiralling into over-indebtedness. The typical cases relate perhaps not so much to consumption of luxury items but to borrowing money for addictions such as alcoholism, drugs and gambling. Risky investments gone wrong can also be the cause of over-indebtedness.

Financial Illiteracy

The inherent idea in borrowing money is the expectation that future income will cover the interest, other related costs and the principal. This is not a simple calculation; it requires financial literacy. In the US, the authors of a report for the President's Advisory Council on Financial Literacy defined financial literacy as "the ability to use knowledge and skills to manage financial resources effectively for a lifetime of financial well-being" (Rogers et al. 2015). In the UK, for example, the alternative term "financial capability" is used by the state, its agencies and researchers.

By definition financial literacy refers to the set of skills and knowledge that allows an individual to make informed and effective decisions with all of their financial resources. The fact that financial products are more numerous and increasingly sophisticated requires personal proficiency in money management, planning and product information to avoid debt problems. Evidence from consumer research on dispersion suggests that many households leave substantial amounts of money on the table by failing to find good deals on loans (Zinman 2015).

Individuals tend, some more and some less, to overestimate their capacity to manage domestic financial resources; meanwhile they are also likely to underestimate the possibility of being affected by negative events such as illness or job loss. Unrealistic expectations are also typical symptoms of psychiatric illnesses. More recent literature points to scarcity as a causal factor harming human functioning among poor individuals (Mullainathan and Shafir 2013). The constant battle with scarce resources to keep up with loan repayments may sap cognitive resources and cause stress and anxiety, which then impairs the quality of decision making and leads to behaviour that may appear reckless to outsiders.

Kilborn (2005) argues that just as lawmakers in the wake of market liberalization have been throwing consumers into the "shark-infested ocean of new borrowing opportunities", so behavioural researchers have been uncovering systematic hindrances to consumers' attempts to swim in this ocean. Behavioural economics has drawn attention to the role played not only by socio-demographic and economic variables, but also by behavioural factors as determinants of the demand for debt and subsequent debt problems. While traditional micro-economists assess decisions relating to debts as a rational calculus, behavioural economists emphasize that household debt is also driven by emotional factors, such as overconfidence, impulsivity in consumption attitudes, social comparison and myopia (Anderloni and Vandone 2011). This is reflected in the fact that many people are failing to plan ahead in their finances and are taking on financial risks without realizing it.

While the traditional *homo economicus* model is postulated on the premise of rational choice, the behaviouristic claim that people act inadvertently. People fail to maximize their own future utility not because they are irrational but because their rationality is "bounded" by documented and consistent biases and mental shortcuts. These "bounds" of rationality affect behaviour particularly in contexts involving many complex variables and ambiguous, unpredictable consequences of any given choice – like consumer borrowing (Kilborn 2005). The inability to perceive the long-run consequences of today's debt decisions may tempt individuals to make "non-rational" borrowing choices, and this may lead them to hold a level of debt that is unsustainable in relation to their earnings. Such decisions may be due to lack of financial literacy or individuals' inability to process effectively information available and, as a result, to evaluate the consequences of indebtedness.

Pointing the individual cause of over-indebtedness to lack of skills is a considerably less moralistic approach than the one which emphasizes debtors' intentional recklessness as a cause of debt problems. A large body of literature has identified psychological features that distinguish those with debt problems from those without problems. Dynamic analyses suggest, however, that many of the differences in psychological variables may be a consequence of being in debt rather than a cause of it (Webley and Nyhus 2001).

A related individual cause of unsustainable debt load is connected to social stigma and shame around incurring debt. This may act as a barrier to enticing honest over-indebted consumers into the system of debt counselling and advice. Not only undeserving debtors keep out of a consumer insolvency system. The moment of truth when announcing one's inability to service financial commitments, either in writing or in person, can be a deeply embarrassing and stigmatizing event (CPEC 2013, p. 168).

There is some research on the gender-specific causes of over-indebtedness (Bull 2007; Betti et al. 2007; Keese 2009; Goode 2009, 2012a; Blomgren et al. 2016, 2017). It is known that there are gender differences in financial literacy (for example Smelser and Swedberg

2005). The gender differences also relate to financial risk taking and distribution of financial tasks between couples and in the financial behaviour that is connected to gender roles.

Unsuccessful Investments

It is possible to make a distinction between the ("productive") households who take out loans for building up assets and the ("unproductive") households who use credit for consumption (see Reifner 2003). For the upwardly mobile, taking on debt enables them to adopt affluent lifestyles and even build up assets. The downwardly mobile economic career involves a mechanism whereby some credit gives access to more credit until it can no longer be sustained. Ultimately, they are excluded from a wide range of life chances and exposed to socio-economic deprivation with no means to store food or to dry clothes, no access to private education and medical facilities (Ford 1988, pp. 184–186).

The affluent act upon social constraints linking material goods to status, while the unemployed, low paid and poor must rely on credit for subsistence (Poppe 2008, p. 30). Low-income households might take credit for other purposes than the better-off; instead of investing in entrepreneurial activity, property and stocks or promoting a consumer lifestyle, they may need to borrow money to cover life necessities and other basic needs like washing machines, mobile phones and television sets. As a result of precarious employment situations, they may also take credit to smooth income fluctuations.

However, the "productive" households may also end up in financial problems if their business and investment loans default with personal liability. When investors and business owners get into financial troubles, lenders routinely ask for extra assets for collateral or surety. If the troubles continue and the debtor defaults on business loans, the liabilities can add up to substantial amounts.

The reasons behind unsuccessful business and investment enterprises are many, and some of them point more towards structural than individual causes. However, the common denominator for failures is that the enterprise was risky from the very start. It is, of course, very difficult to objectively make a distinction between overly risky and normally risky investment since all investments come with risks. To reduce their own risk the creditors often demand personal guarantee from the debtors whose project is deemed high risk. Behavioural economics observations on overconfidence, impulsivity in investment attitudes and myopia may explain risky investments as a cause of over-indebtedness (Anderloni and Vandone 2011).

Reckless Spending

Consumer recklessness is connected with the borrower's alleged tendency to imitate others, overlooking the risks involved in lending, and borrowers' materialistic values. A hopeless financial situation may also create a moral hazard, especially in those countries where relatively easy consumer insolvency processes are available. If there is no way to pay off overdue debts, the household may start piling up debt while anticipating that everything will be eventually written off through insolvency proceedings.

Caplovitz makes an important distinction between borrowers' *inability* to pay and *unwillingness* to pay, and admits that irresponsible behaviour on the debtor's side may contribute to debt problems. In his sample Caplovitz (1974, pp. 85–90) estimates the proportion of irresponsible debtors at around 5 per cent. This category included debt problems caused by personal qualities like "bad faith", forgetfulness, refusal to pay for merchandize that was stolen or broken, and economic disorder. Bad faith related to cases where the debtor just lost interest in paying.

A qualitative interview study in the UK determined than payment of debts is dependent on both ability to pay and commitment to pay (Dominy and Kempson 2003). In some cases, people have a genuine dispute with their creditor and are withholding payment until the dispute is resolved. Unpaid bills and irregular payment may also relate to cases where people are disorganized in their approach to bill payment. As cases of bad intent and unwillingness to pay Dominy and Kempson list people holding back money on principle: withholding payment of debts to ex-partners; attempts to work the system to see if payment can be avoided altogether; and running away from responsibilities by blaming the creditors for debt problems. People may withhold money on principled belief that they are not receiving a satisfactory service or that they are getting poor value for money from their creditor. The group of ex-partners withholding payment includes those who retain responsibility for paying some or all of the bills in their former family home but withhold these payments. There are also debtors who are "working the system" by deliberately and routinely waiting until late in the debt recovery cycle before paying just about all their bills. People in this group usually have a long history of arrears and county court judgments on a variety of commitments. Finally, Dominy and Kempson identified a group of people who are "ducking responsibility" by spending freely and owing very large sums in consumer credit.

Non-payment is sometimes related to changes in repayment norms and attitudes. Gross and Souleles (2001) relate the upward trend in the number of US bankruptcies during the late 1990s to declines in default costs, including social, information and legal costs. The study showed that even after controlling for risk composition and other economic fundamentals, the propensity to default significantly increased between 1995 and 1997. The authors suggested that it has become less stigmatizing to default on bills and financial commitments, and as a consequence socially easier to declare bankruptcy. A Norwegian survey found that immoral attitudes and unwillingness to pay were the main causes behind the rising numbers of late payments from 1997 to 2004; in other words unwillingness to pay was a more important reason for late payment than inability to pay (Gulbrandsen 2005). According to this research report payment neglect was especially common among people in their twenties. However, the incidences of "abuse" in existing personal insolvency systems can be overstated.

Immorality may not necessarily relate to debtors' behaviour towards the creditors but to the purpose of the credit. These cases concern gambling credits, loans to buy drugs and reparations for criminal conduct. As far as the immoral behaviour is linked with addiction there is an inherent tendency for the debt problem to get out of hand. Barron et al.'s (2002) analysis with US counties covering the period 1993–1999 shows significant (but small) increases in the number of personal bankruptcy filings after the introduction of casino gambling at the county level.

While Caplovitz's (1974) empirical measurement principles can be questioned, it is noteworthy that the scope of immorality among the debtors was limited to a small minority, while the public image of default-debtors is sometimes dominated by descriptions of misbehaviour. Gerardi et al. (2015) find that in the US 15 per cent of mortgage defaults may be "strategic". With a comparatively very liberal insolvency regime strategic default and moral hazard are supposedly less likely in the more conservative insolvency regimes. The widespread use of debt advice and counselling services speaks also against immorality as a central cause of over-indebtedness. In the CPEC study the over-indebted individuals reported seeking advice or taking measures to alleviate their debt problems. These findings support the conclusion that most consumers find the experience of over-indebtedness distressing and are eager to repay their debts. If a multitude of consumers were engaged in strategic default, why would they waste their time on debt counselling services, rather than engaging with the consumer insolvency procedure or out-of-court settlement directly (CPEC 2013, p. 168)?

Reckless behaviour is not necessarily a sign of faults in an individual's character. It can be related to general social and psychological factors that reduce an individual's capacity to evaluate the consequences of his/her consumption, investment and borrowing decisions Behavioural economics has identified several biases – such as an overconfidence bias, inter-temporal balancing of utility, locus of control or habit persistence – as contributory factors to over-indebtedness. Gathergood (2012a) showed that lack of self-control was positively associated with non-payment of consumer credit and self-reported excessive financial burdens of debt among UK consumers. According to this study, individuals with self-control problems make disproportionate use of quick-access credit products which facilitate impulse-driven purchases.

Apart from unexceptional circumstances, excess consumption financed through borrowing can be considered a cause of over-indebtedness. According to the reckless spending view, people borrow money to finance irresponsible spending and lifestyle behaviours, which leads to unsustainable debt and eventually to over-indebtedness. At the time when credit markets were strictly controlled, causal explanations where the blame was pinned on the default-debtors were common. They carried moralistic undertones suggesting that debt problems largely emerge from reckless behaviour or ill-intent. Liberalization of financial markets has brought lender liability to the fore, but has not completely silenced the debate on consumer recklessness as a cause of over-indebtedness. Economic crises lead naturally to reactions of moral judgment and outcry. Public opinion turns against homeowners who borrowed too much. Mian and Sufi (2015a, p. 59) consider these types of attitudes counterproductive since everybody will suffer if a large number of people start pulling back household spending.

Default-debtors are expected to act in accordance with any legal statute that applies to the particular situations they are in (Poppe 2008, p. 13). Poppe, who interviewed Norwegian default-debtors suffering from debt problems for more than 15 years, demonstrated vividly that they do not always comply; but instead, creditors often complain about default-debtors who make poor decisions and behave financially imprudently, for example defaulting on renegotiated repayment schedules.

However, behaviour which appears irrational or irresponsible may find explanation through the social context people with financial problems are facing. The basic idea of this approach is that people who have not experienced poverty or over-indebtedness should not judge people going through those hardships. Through analysis of 20 qualitative interviews with people who suffered severe debt problems, Christian Poppe concluded that the reason some of their actions seemed stupid, irrational or even immoral was that they were defending their social lives – for example through serving "debts of honour" from friends and relatives – while neglecting claims from banks and public officials.

In the same vein, Matthew Desmond (2016), an anthropologist from the US who collected data by living in a trailer park in Milwaukee, asserts that poor people live with compounded financial and social limitations. No amount of good behaviour or self-control would allow them to lift themselves out of poverty; they would not climb out of it "even if they pinched every penny", so they chose not to do so. Desmond described instances when poor people try to "survive in colour" and to "season the suffering with pleasure":

> To Sammy, Pastor Daryl, and others, Larraine was poor because she threw money away. But the reverse was more true. Larraine threw money away because she was poor. ... They would get a little high or have a drink or do a bit of gambling or acquire a television. They might buy lobster on food stamps. (Desmond 2016, p. 219)

This situation may resemble moral hazard, but it is not motivated through economical calculation but rather through seeking identity and meaning.

Bad luck

Dutch scholar Wim van Oorschot (2000) divides the perceptions for causes of poverty into three categories: societal blame, individual blame and bad luck (see also van Oorschot and Halman 2000). Studying the financial careers of over-indebted individuals, Poppe (2008) concluded that, in his sample of 20 informants, bad luck was the most typical explanation the default-debtors gave for their debt problems. However, as an objective cause of over-indebtedness, bad luck should refer to conditions which are beyond the control of any identifiable actor.

With bad luck, van Oorschot and Poppe referred to remote processes totally outside their control which resulted in negative changes to their financial careers. These events related to structural factors driving up the cost of debts. An illustrative example was given by one of Poppe's interviewees, who referred to the economic crisis at the end of the 1980s and early 1990s in Norway: "I moved out of Oslo and started a boat building company. The first two or three months or so we were doing just fine. But then came the stock market collapse, and our market died over-night. The bank named me their most unfortunate customer" (Poppe 2008, p. 188).

Over-indebtedness can also result from surety. Surety is the guarantee of the debts of one party by another. That means a person assumes the responsibility of paying the debt in case the debtor defaults. People tend to act as surety for their relatives or friends. The original debtor may encounter unexpected misfortune, even death. In this case, the creditor turns to surety for payment, which he or she may not be able to meet. Again, it is difficult to say whether this case falls into the category of bad luck or if a person should have given more consideration before assuming the responsibility of paying the debt in case the debtor defaults.

DECREASE IN INCOMES: STRUCTURAL FACTORS

Households with high incomes may end up in debt problems, for example, as a result of business bankruptcy or bad personal investment, and may not escape over-indebtedness even if they are able to sustain a high level of income before default (sometimes also after default). The debt problems are, however, much more common among those with middle or low incomes and among those with no assets. Income protection offered by the welfare state in the incidence of unemployment or sickness is supposedly a major factor in over-indebtedness. The same goes for public services such as education and health care. In some countries people might get caught with high medical debts or student loans as a result of lost earnings during recuperation or studies, while other countries provide income replacement during illness or study grants, which reduces the need for study loans. Also, labour market policies regulating for example minimum wages and general taxation policies have an impact on households' daily choices between paying debts and other bills and spending the money on food, clothes and other basic needs (Poppe 2008, p. 36). Low- and middle-income households most often need to spend the largest share of their incomes on housing.

Welfare State

The traditional idea of welfare state social policies is to protect individuals and households against social risks. The so-called old social risks relate directly to incidences where an individual's capacity to earn income from the market, either as a wage-labourer or entrepreneur, are weakened. The most common risks include giving birth and caring for a child, education, unemployment, sickness, work disability and old age. The very existence of social protection in terms of income replacement has facilitated the democratization of debts. Families with low incomes and precarious work situations have been able to access credit by demonstrating ability to repay even in the event of unemployment or sickness.

Welfare state types are traditionally analysed in the light of the division of labour between central institutions which provide social protection for individuals and families. The institutions are the state (or the state and municipalities), non-governmental organizations (religious and other), the family and markets (cf. Esping-Andersen 1990; Korpi and Palme 1998). Constructing typologies or categories of welfare states characterized social policy research during the last two decades. Esping-Andersen's *Three Worlds of Welfare Capitalism* (1990) launched an avalanche of typologies. Interest in cross-national comparisons has produced a number of theoretical models attempting to capture or summarize the similarities and differences in public policies employed in Western industrial countries. The models have proved surprisingly robust.

The Anglo-Saxon (or liberal) tradition relies on targeted benefits and overlooks the role of income transfers and public services. The discussion revolves around morals and need. Such countries, represented here by the US and the UK, stress heavily means-tested cash benefits in accordance with the British income maintenance tradition. Public policy is dominated by the negative conceptions of government intervention and the detrimental incentive structures that social policy may create; social programmes are sometimes seen as an incentive to failure (Murray 1984). Programmes are targeted at disadvantaged groups like single mothers, but the benefit levels are inadequate to lift these groups out of poverty. In-work poverty is also common. Apart from the marginal populations, the market is the decisive factor in the well-being of individuals. This model has resulted in high levels of poverty. High medical costs (in the US) and tuition fees, medical debts and student debts can lead to over-indebtedness (Sullivan et al. 2000). Tax policies favour homeownership, and with meagre subsidies for public housing markets are clearly divided into owner-occupied and renter sectors.

The Central European (or conservative) tradition emphasizes the role of the breadwinner and the family in guaranteeing the well-being of individuals. Public policy in these countries (here Germany and the Netherlands) has been affected by the principle of subsidiarity and Catholic traditions (Kersbergen 1995). Key public services, such as education and health care, are privately produced but publicly financed. Those not covered through employment-based protection may need to rely on poor-level services and poor income protection. Since social benefits are tied to (male) employment, partnership dissolution puts women especially at risk of poverty.

The Nordic (or social-democratic) tradition stresses the role of the government in providing social security, which means both comprehensive income transfers and publicly financed and produced services (Hiilamo and Kangas 2013). The basic idea of the Nordic model (with Finland and Norway as examples here) is to pursue universal welfare state policies, which means that public programmes, services and transfers are designed to serve everyone living in the country. All the Nordic countries have large, tax-funded public welfare sectors and extensive social legislation that provides a safety-net "from cradle to grave". After a deep recession in the early 1990s, the Nordic welfare states were less universal, less generous and more conditional than in the late 1980s. However, the Nordic welfare model was still distinct and fared well in comparison with other welfare state models. Poverty and inequality rates are low, income mobility – be it short term or intergenerational – was high. The 1990 crisis showed that the universal welfare state model was able to absorb macro-economic shocks and stabilize living conditions when needed (Kiander and Vartia 2011). With abundant resources in the sovereign oil fund, Norway was best insulated against the Global economic crises; but Finland also chose not to introduce cuts in public spending and to maintain the comprehensive welfare state benefits which were urgently needed during the time of crisis.

Regardless of what kind of approach is used to categorize welfare states, the countries discussed in this book tend to end up in the same categories. However, both Germany and the Netherlands have implemented policies that are typical of the Nordic countries – for example, measures to promote female labour force participation. Female employment gives couples more leeway in facing financial problems.

The lack of income support from the welfare state makes individuals and families more vulnerable to income shocks that may lead to debt problems and over-indebtedness. It is very difficult to assess to what degree this is the case since more liberal debt discharge policies which were discussed in the previous chapter may compensate for the poorer welfare state programmes in Anglo-Saxon countries vis-à-vis the Nordic countries, for example. A country study by Fisher and Lyon (2006) showed that, when controlling for different years and state-fixed effects as well as socio-demographic variables, a 10 per cent increase in unemployment benefits led to a 2.2 per cent decrease in the bankruptcy filing rate in the US. The result speaks for the effect of welfare state policies to prevent over-indebtedness.

Labour Market

Most households use earnings to repay debts. Restructuring processes in the labour market may lead to redundancy and reduced incomes for many households, and thereby contribute to over-indebtedness (Poppe 2008, p. 38). Labour markets are subject both to structural and seasonal changes. The outstanding example of the latter category is increase in unemployment as a consequence of recession.

Since the 1980s "flexibilization", a term referring to shifts in the types of jobs offered – from traditional full-time and long-term employment to flexible contracts – has been a dominant trend in the labour market of the rich nations.

The economic globalization has exported especially manufacturing jobs to countries offering a cheaper labour force. That has also weakened labour unions, which have traditionally defended workers' income protection. The average production worker's wage has not increased in some countries, and in all countries job contracts have become more uncertain. For example, in neoliberal employment regimes of the US and the UK many employees have found themselves in a downward spiral, subject to frequent job losses and re-employment at lower salaries (Poppe 2008, p. 38).

The labour markets are also characterized by job polarization, where both high-pay and low-pay jobs increase in numbers while traditional middle-income jobs are vanishing. The insecurity in labour markets makes it harder especially for low-income households to manage debts, especially in the US and UK, while the reduced demand for labour as a consequence of the Global economic crises increased over-indebtedness also in Finland.

DECREASE IN INCOMES: INDIVIDUAL FACTORS

Income-related individual risk factors for over-indebtedness can be approached from a life-cycle perspective which recognizes the fact that during certain phases of life and life situations, changes in income weigh more than during others. In his classic 1901 study on poverty in York, Seebohm Rowntree (1871–1954) observed that poverty was linked to age and family formation in a cyclical fashion (Figure 3.1). The first poverty incidence was experienced during "childhood", when parents had many dependants to feed and when the earnings of one person were not enough to meet the needs of all family members. Poverty eased in the "youth phase", when the young person left home and began to earn his/her own living. Economically, the situation became worse again when he/she got married and had children. This stage of the early middle-age years – the "family phase" – continued until the children grew up, began to contribute to the family income and then, one by one, left home. At this point, he/she entered an economically easier "empty nest" period. This stage would last until old age brought on a lower capacity for work.

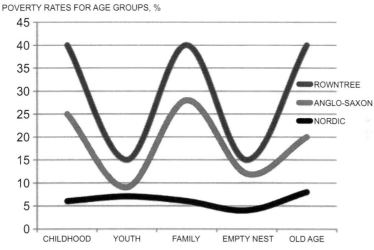

POVERTY RATES FOR AGE GROUPS, %

Source: Hiilamo and Kangas (2013).

Figure 3.1 Rowntree's poverty cycle in York (1899) and the 2010s' cycle in Nordic and Anglo-Saxon welfare states

The causal factor in the poverty cycle was the capacity to work. The development of the modern welfare state has reduced dependency on work income (sometimes called decommodification) (Esping-Andersen 1990; Hiilamo and Kangas 2013). This means that in the event of unemployment, sickness or old age, individuals and households can sustain a decent living standard. As discussed earlier, this has made households more resilient to income shocks and debt problems related to them, while it has also encouraged households to increase debt burden and thereby increased the risk of over-indebtedness. Previous research has demonstrated that unemployment is a significant risk for over-indebtedness (Fondeville et al. 2010; CPEC 2013). A study by the European Central Bank showed that the likelihood of being over-indebted in the euro area is clearly higher among those who are inactive or unemployed compared with those who are employed (Caju et al. 2016).

These results were stable across different over-indebtedness indicators and specifications.

Another central feature of the modern welfare state is that public services have been developed to replace unpaid care work. That concerns most prominently care for small children, and disabled and frail elderly populations. In this respect, there are major differences across welfare state types. The Nordic welfare state model guarantees subjective rights to child day care and also includes institutional care for disabled and frail elderly people, with heavily subsidized prices or for free (Hiilamo and Kangas 2013). This means that caring for a child, a disabled family member or a frail elderly person is seldom a cause of over-indebtedness in Finland or Norway, for example. Lack of public care services in the UK and the US can lead to a situation where a sudden need for care will lower household incomes and could lead to over-indebtedness. Public care services insulate two-adult households from over-indebtedness also through the support of the dual earner model. It is unlikely that calculation for a sudden need for unpaid care work, depending on welfare state arrangements, will incentivize households to take out more or fewer loans. However, it is obvious that the dominant dual-earner model, which is also gaining ground in the Netherlands and even in Germany, will encourage couples to obtain larger mortgages.

In economics, the life-cycle hypothesis (LCH) of saving assumes that young people have low income and savings, and consequently borrow more, but then save more during middle age and finally spend more during retirement (Ando and Modigliani 1963). The theory has been called into question with increasing over-indebtedness among both young and old cohorts (Montgomerie 2013). The literature shows, however, that reduction in work income is still one of the strongest predictors of over-indebtedness. In a comprehensive survey of previous literature, individual statistical analysis and consumer and stakeholder interviews, CPEC (2013, p. 7) confirmed that the lower the income, the greater the risk of over-indebtedness, even after controlling for other factors. Over-indebtedness is most common among households with disposable incomes of less than 60 per cent of the national median. These households are also the ones most dramatically affected by economic crises. Using data on influenza outbreaks in 83 metropolitan areas in the US, Houle et al. (2015) demonstrated that there was a small but statistically significant association between credit card and mortgage defaults and influenza outbreaks. The result indicates that exogenous health shocks (such as influenza) can act as a driver for credit defaults.

The role of individual social risks as a cause of over-indebtedness is highlighted also in the results from the 2008 European Union Statistics on Income and Living Conditions (EU-SILC) household panel, which included a special ad hoc module on indebtedness (Fondeville et al. 2010). Comprehensive analysis confirming earlier results showed that people who have been involved in marriage break-up, as well as lone parents, have high levels of debt relative to income. Those who rent their accommodation are more prone to have high debt levels than those who own the house in which they live. The results also showed that a sudden drop in income seems to be an important cause of a high level of indebtedness throughout the EU. Such a drop was in many cases a result of job loss in the year leading up to the survey in 2008, when the economic downturn began to hit EU Member States. Kempson et al. (2004, p. 32) used an over-indebtedness survey in the UK (undertaken in 2002) to study the causes and impact of arrears. They assert that the possible factors contributing to the increased risk of arrears among all households are housing tenure, age group, drops in income, having active credit commitments and whether a current account was being used to manage money.

Caplovitz (1979), who studied economic downturn in the 1970s in the US, used the term "voluntary over-extension" to describe previously unproblematic credit that had become unmanageable due to decrease in incomes. Voluntary over-extension is not only related to unemployment but also to other types of social risks which reduce capacity to work and earn incomes. They include sickness, disability, partnership dissolution and old age. The social risks the welfare state is aimed to protect against are never fully compensated. The risks cause sudden drops in incomes which may lead to over-indebtedness. The severity of the risk with regard to debt problems can be simply assessed against the loss of income resulting from the risk. There are also special individual circumstances which may reduce incomes. The obvious example is imprisonment in the US.

INCREASE IN THE COST OF LIVING: STRUCTURAL FACTORS

The ramifications of social risks may not only stem from loss of income, but also from increased expenditures. Caplovitz's evidence from the effect of economic downturn in the 1970s in the US showed that the ability to withstand changes in the cost of absolutely necessary consumption varied across social divisions. In *Making Ends Meet* Caplovitz (1979) described how recession with high unemployment rates and inflation causing escalating expenditures forced particularly poor and blue-collar households into financial difficulties. The obvious reason was the unequal distribution of resources along traditional class divides.

Rises in the cost of living constrain indebted households' capacity to service debts, and thereby contribute to over-indebtedness. This is true especially for those households which have long struggled with small incomes and mounting debts. Changes in the consumer price index measure the rise in cost of living for average households. That is a rough measure and may not fully capture the changes in indebted households' capacity to manage debts. People with low incomes tend to spend, in relative terms, more money on food than average-income households. In the CPEC study the main concerns for stakeholders as a cause of over-indebtedness included utility bills, followed by housing costs and other costs, including food and transport. Other areas of expenditure such as childcare and other child-related costs, health care costs, education and insurance were seen as less important causes of over-indebtedness. The consumer interviewees referred, as causes of their financial difficulties, most frequently to utility costs, the general costs of living, housing costs and childcare or child-related costs. Health care and education costs were also mentioned. In Germany, interviewees most frequently referred to housing costs, followed by the general costs of living and childcare or child-related costs. Almost half of the interviewed households in the UK considered the general costs of living to be a cause of their financial difficulties, specifying utility and childcare or child-related costs (CPEC 2013, p. 139).

As regards utility costs the CPEC (2013, p. 36) study focused expressly on electricity, water supply, gas and other fuels, and tele-communications. The study found that across the EU there has been a rapid rise in utility prices in recent years compared to the general cost of living, while prices for telecom services have seen a general decline. During the post-crisis period (2007–2011), the electricity price index, for example, increased five times more than income per capita, while the liquid fuels index increased by nearly ten times. The correlation analysis showed an association with frequency of arrears in utility costs and various indices of utility costs for the 27 Member States (CPEC 2013, p. 9). In terms of changes in the pre- and post-2008 crisis periods, increases in perception of heavy burdens due to housing costs were highest in Estonia, Latvia, Malta, Lithuania and Denmark, while the level of problems decreased significantly in Bulgaria and modestly in Germany, Italy and the Netherlands. Cost of living is also driven by demographic factors. In all countries discussed here more people tend to live alone and not enjoy economies of scale for bigger households. People live longer, which also makes elderly populations susceptible to debt problems. On the other hand, families have become smaller, which reduces the cost of living.

INCREASE IN THE COST OF LIVING: INDIVIDUAL FACTORS

Caplovitz (1974) calls "involuntary over-extension" a situation where households experienced some kind of unexpected expenditure like medical bills, hospitalization or the death of a relative, unforeseen car repairs and telephone bills resulting in an increase in debt burden. The expansion of debts can also happen less suddenly, for example through general jumps in energy, food or transportation prices. In these cases, we would consider the change as structural. However, living expenses may also increase as a result of changes in individual circumstances.

The fact that low-income households are more vulnerable to economic problems, including over-indebtedness, is reflected in the fact that over-indebtedness is more concentrated among people renting their home. Owner-occupied housing is associated with a lower risk of over-indebtedness. This is, of course, more clearly the case with those who own their home outright than with those with mortgages. Under financially compounded circumstances indebted households may not have the means available to average households to resist increases in the cost of living. For example, they might not be able to change apartment if the rent is increased, since they might not have enough money for a rent guarantee.

Individual Social Risks with a Bearing on Expenditure

Severe and/or long-term physical and mental illness may come with increased expenditures to cover expensive medicines, rehabilitation and disability. The effects of these conditions on household expenditure are not completely mitigated even in the most developed welfare states. The effects are more pronounced, though, in countries with poor health insurance such as the US. In the CPEC (2013, pp. 148–149) study focusing on Europe only a few of the interviewees mentioned health care costs as a cause of over-indebtedness. Not surprisingly, neither health care nor education was mentioned as playing a significant role in levels of over-indebtedness, mainly because they are either free at the point of use or the costs are comparatively low. However, health care costs were singled out as being important in the Netherlands. The high cost of education was mentioned by stakeholders in the UK (CPEC 2013,

p. 148). In contrast, in the US, medical debt is a major cause of over-indebtedness (Sullivan et al. 2000).

According to the life-cycle theory, households use credit to balance needs and income across the life course. The needs are directly linked to family composition. As Rowntree (1901) pointed out, young children increase costs, as do partnership dissolutions. Two-adult families can combine incomes and enjoy economies of scale, for example in the purchase of accommodation and vehicles. These factors are important when households are hit by economic problems. Consequently, the demographic trend from two-adult families to one-adult families has made households more vulnerable to debt problems.

Empirical results from EU-SILC show that households with children are more likely to have high ratios of debt to income than those without children; and that older people of 65 and over are less likely to have high levels of debt than other age groups (Fondeville et al. 2010). The incidence of high debt levels does not tend to vary much with age among the population of working age. Research has also shown, again just as Rowntree predicted, that the number of children in a household signifi-cantly increases the risk of being in financial difficulties. Results from EU-SILC data demonstrate that respondents with no dependants had consistently less than half the level of total arrears than respondents with dependants (Fondeville et al. 2010).

However, even the most comprehensive welfare states fail to address all possible social risks. One of those risks is divorce and relationship breakdown. Previous research has shown that lone parents are at greater risk than two-parent families. They are particularly disadvantaged since they lose more in terms of economies of scale, especially in childcare (both day care fees and value of unpaid care work). Welfare states compensate for this condition to varying degrees with social transfers, including housing assistance, child allowance and subsidized day care fee schedules. In the conservative and liberal welfare state regimes, the common wisdom was that every woman is only one divorce away from bankruptcy. Policies have changed over the last few decades, but divorce continues as a major reason for debt problems. That is the case especially among families with small children who demand care and reduce opportunities for paid labour (CPEC 2013). Both bad health and divorce not only cut incomes but also come with extra costs (depending on the health care system). In the case of divorce, both partners need extra income to compensate for the loss of economies of scale. If a former couple has owned the house or apartment together, the property has to be sold or the remaining partner needs extra credit to cover the missing share of the mortgage.

Ford (1988, pp. 109–111), who interviewed 40 households with mort-gage arrears, observed that not only divorce and partnership dissolution but also disputes and lack of communication worsen debt problems. Sometimes after years of juggling, "back-pedalling" or "robbing Peter to pay Paul" the couples slide to the point where these strategies can no longer balance incomes and expenditures. Couples facing aggravated financial strain must make decisions on, for example, which bills to pay and which bills to leave unpaid; which money-consuming activities, including hobbies, to continue and which to discontinue. These expend-iture choices can be a major source of conflict. Debt problems may also reveal different levels of commitment and different preferences for owner-occupation, couple's individual contributions to household incomes and to agreements concerning the use of money in the house-hold. Ford (1988, p. 111) described couples' disputes over the use of financial resources where arrears were "a way of making a point", "gaining advantage" or "forcing a desired course of action". Ford suggests that "bad debts may be the way one party pressurizes the other, particularly in order to gain economic resources".

Unfortunate Circumstances

Besides all other structural and individual causes described above there are unfortunate events outside the control of the individual which might increase costs of living (or decrease incomes). Unfortunate circumstances point to a complex class of misfortunes which cannot be included in the other categories of over-indebtedness causes. Ford (1988, pp. 113–116) counts home repairs and maintenance as important factors for expend-iture increase and routes to arrears. This is especially relevant for low-income households who often purchase older and cheaper property which is in constant need of improvement. Desmond (2016) describes trailer park owners' strategies to sell trailers to tenants for one dollar to avoid responsibility for repairs. The tenants often get into arrears as a result of costly renovations which are necessary to keep the trailers habitable. Mold in houses is a major problem in Finland.

It is problematic to study quantitatively the role of unfortunate circumstances in over-indebtedness. It is very difficult to say, for example, who caused a stock market collapse or a Global economic crisis. The most obvious cases of unfortunate circumstances relate to natural disasters. Economic recessions are not natural disasters, even if many times those most culpable for causing them claim they are. An individual could perceive a circumstance as a misfortune, even though it could be entirely attributed to personal failures. On the other hand, unfortunate circumstances could be attributed to known structural factors which are influenced by an identifiable group of decision-makers.

Are personal accounts of blaming unfortunate circumstances for economic problems trustworthy causal explanations? This remains an open question. It is not possible to operationalize unfortunate circumstances, and there are no qualitative studies which would have tried to shed light on the problem. Anecdotes of unfortunate circumstances have the power to demonstrate a credible causal mechanism from unfortunate circumstances to over-indebtedness. Hardly anybody would intentionally become over-indebted, and every individual case of over-indebtedness involves unfortunate circumstances; but at this point we may not come up with a generalizable estimate on the prevalence of unfortunate circumstances as a causal factor in over-indebtedness.

COUNTRY-SPECIFIC CAUSES OF OVER-INDEBTEDNESS

What are the most important structural or individual causes of over-indebtedness in each country? Gutiérrez-Nieto et al. (2017) surveyed both individual and expert opinions on the causes of over-indebtedness in Spain. They found that individuals emphasize external adverse shocks (such as economic crisis), internal adverse shocks (such as unemployment) and financial institutions' pressure on debtors, while the experts tend to blame the individuals' lack of financial literacy and tendency for overconsumption to maintain lifestyles to keep up with their peers. It is clear that, for instance, real estate speculation and subprime mortgages to poor people in the run-up to the Global economic crises created a housing bubble which burst, leaving hundreds of thousands with negative equity. It created huge ramifications not only in the US but also in Europe.

It is also true that the financial industry, with developed marketing technologies and unscrupulous lending practices, has contributed enormously to over-indebtedness across the Western countries. The recessions and the financial industry operate in the context of global capitalist markets. However, each country has its own narrative of economic and housing market crises with national decision-makers and path-dependencies. Also, the globalized economy and inadequately regulated financial markets have greatly contributed to, if not created, the over-indebtedness problem in the studied countries. In the CPEC (2013, p. 156) study 9 out of 10 of the stakeholders interviewed agreed that that macro-economic factors are among the most important causes of financial difficulties.

Several studies on over-indebtedness have included a number of variables which allow us to assess the most important individual causes of over-indebtedness. A study by Caju et al. (2016) showed that structural factors matter for the prevalence of over-indebtedness in the euro area. They found that the probability of being over-indebted was higher in countries where the foreclosure costs (in case of default on mortgage debt) were higher. They interpreted the results to suggest that increased costs of foreclosure incentivize lenders to ask for higher interest rates from riskier groups like the unemployed or the retired. However, they did not find an association between financial regulation or unemployment insurance systems and over-indebtedness in accounting for differences across labour market status. However, better information on borrowers appeared to decrease the likelihood of being over-indebted for the retired group. By using debt enforcement as a measure of over-indebtedness Oksanen et al. (2015) showed that male gender, low socio-economic status, age, marital status, number of children and prior criminal convictions were associated with debt problems in Finland. Interestingly, they found that income was not associated with the amount of outstanding private receivables, indicating that debt problems do not only boil down to social stratification and poverty.

It would be tempting to relate the causes of over-indebtedness to particular personal insolvency regimes or welfare state regimes. However, in the absence of comparable data we have to be satisfied with some general observations. In Germany, special legislation on over-indebtedness statistics (*Überschuldungsstatistikgesetz*) was passed and became a law in 2012 (Statistisches Bundesamt 2017). The data collection is carried out through officially approved counselling centres where counselling is free of charge if the attendee meets the eligibility criterion for receiving debt and insolvency counselling. The criterion is "being in serious financial difficulties". The law allows, for example, collection of reasons for over-indebtedness through 1400 legislated debt counselling service providers, who provide counselling for those individuals and households with severe debt problems.

Since this data comes very close to the definition of over-indebtedness in this study, it is useful to report some of the findings for the year 2016 (Figure 3.2). The providers participated voluntarily in data collection. For example, as many as 461 providers provided data on about 118 000 over-indebted individuals. This means the data is not completely representative due to the fact that only a fraction of debt counselling providers participated in the data collection, and there is no data on those over-indebted individuals who sought advice from those providers.

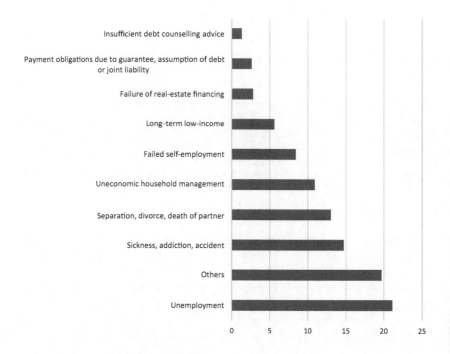

Source: Statistisches Bundesamt (2017).

Figure 3.2   Causes of over-indebtedness among debt counselling clients in Germany in 2016 (%)

In the German data, unemployment stands out as the most important cause of individual over-indebtedness. If we also take into account the category of "failed self-employment", labour market related causes accounted for almost one-third of all debt counselling cases. The data from earlier years (2008–2011) is not totally comparable over the year. It shows, however, that unemployment was even more significant in the years right after the Global economic crisis. By household type, unemployment was most the common cause of over-indebtedness among single men (24 per cent).

The institutional design of the welfare state conditions how individuals in a country are protected from misfortunes in the labour market. The breakdown of most important causes of over-indebtedness is unavoidably dependent on the categories used for the study (see Ramsay 2017, pp. 19–22). However, an influential study from the US also found that employment problems (67.5 per cent) were the most important reason for consumer bankruptcies, followed by divorce (21.1 per cent) and medical bills (19.3 per cent) (Sullivan et al. 2000).

In the CPEC (2013, p. 8) study, statistical analysis showed that unemployment levels as well as increases in unemployment were associated with an increase in all types of arrears, while increases in real adjusted gross disposable income of households were also strongly and significantly associated with lower frequencies of arrears. Also, interviewed stakeholders and consumers considered drops in income caused by unemployment to be among the most important causes of household over-indebtedness.

The category of sickness, addiction and accident also plays a major role in identified causes of over-indebtedness in Germany. So does partnership dissolution, which is a new social risk and not very well recognized in the welfare state programmes. In the German data three categories – uneconomic household management, failure of real estate financing and payment obligations due to guarantee – relate to financial literacy. They account for 16 per cent of the cases. This share has remained stable between 2008 and 2016. Failure of real estate financing is a minor category, but interesting for the fact that in this category the overdue debt is clearly highest (on average 133 211 euros as opposed to 31 613 euros for all causes in 2016). In the CPEC (2013, p. 93) study nearly two-thirds of all stakeholders chose "incapacity to deal with financial products" and/or "lack of money management skills" as being among the most important causes of over-indebtedness. That surely reflects an individualized and even a paternalistic view of over-indebtedness, but may also echo the fact that financial products have become ever more complex and difficult to understand.

Given the comprehensive network of public services and income transfers we would then expect that within the Nordic welfare states of Finland and Norway individual characteristics, economic behaviour and lifestyle choices – that is, excessive consumption or short-sighted economic decisions – would be more important causes of over-indebtedness than in less developed welfare states. Poppe et al. (2016) reviewed causes of over-indebtedness in a sample of 100 individual debt settlement cases registered at the court in Oslo. Surprisingly, health problems were the most commonly expressed cause (45 per cent of cases), followed by low income (36 per cent), business bankruptcy (35 per cent), overconsumption (32 per cent), relationship break-up (27 per cent) and loss of property/surety (19 per cent). On average, each case resulted from 2.3 causal processes.

All six countries discussed in this book are interconnected to the global capitalist system where no participant is completely isolated from outside shocks. Of course, some countries are more resilient than others. The Nordic countries of Finland and Norway have developed comprehensive welfare systems to protect citizens from social risks. That holds true to some extent also for over-indebtedness. However, these countries have small and open economies which are particularly vulnerable to changes in the global markets. Norway, with its huge sovereign oil fund, is better protected than Finland.

In the absence of comparative research, it is impossible to directly point out country-specific causes of over-indebtedness. We must suffice with a draft outline of causes which can be taken merely as assumptions to be tested in future research (see Table 3.2). As opposed to European countries, medical bills cause over-indebtedness in the US. That is also the case with other social risks such as unemployment and old age. This is the result of failures by the welfare state to provide universal access to health care and other programmes for families and individuals to protect against social risks. The failures of welfare state are also reflected in high tuition fees and defaulted student loans. The experiences from the Global economic crises, when subprime mortgages became prevalent in the US, indicate that economic illiteracy is an important individual cause of over-indebtedness in the US (Mian and Sufi 2015a). The research evidence from the UK indicates that over-indebtedness is related to labour market structures and low pay, which is reflected in the high levels of in-work poverty in the UK (Giesselmann 2015).

As described above, labour market risks are also important causes of over-indebtedness in Germany. The peculiar tendency in the Netherlands to favour large mortgages poses a special risk to consumers there (OECD 2017a). In Finland, weak regulation created a persistent payday loan industry (Valkama and Muttilainen 2008). Tighter usury regulation was not able to prevent the industry from moving into instalment loans with very high interest rates (Majamaa et al. 2017). Limited or very limited access to consumers is a major cause of over-indebtedness in the continental European and Nordic countries. As to individual causes of over-indebtedness, previous research shows that changes in family structure and uneconomic household management are important causes in Germany (Statistisches Bundesamt 2017), while there is some evidence in Norway pointing to reckless spending behaviour (Gulbrandsen 2005).

Table 3.2   Country-specific structural and individual causes of over-indebtedness in six countries

Country	Structural causes	Individual causes
US	Weak welfare state	Financial illiteracy
UK	In-work poverty	
Germany	Unemployment Limited possibilities for debt discharge	Separation Uneconomic household management
Netherlands	Sizeable mortgages Very limited possibilities for debt discharge	
Finland	Payday loans Limited possibilities for debt discharge	
Norway	Limited possibilities for debt discharge	Reckless spending Health problems

4. Consequences of over-indebtedness

Bankruptcy was a turning point in Rembrandt s life. He lost his house, a mark of his professional standing; and his long-time lover, Hendrickje Stoffels (1626–1663), their daughter Cornelia and Titus, his son from his first marriage, had to move to a modest dwelling in the outskirts of the city (Crenshaw 2006). In addition, Rembrandt had to give up his impressive collection of paintings, prints and drawings, antiquities and rarities, and naturalia. As a result of the bankruptcy, Rembrandt was also unable to operate as an independent professional. The authorities and Rembrandt's creditors were eventually accommodating, but the Amsterdam painters' guild introduced a new rule that no one in Rembrandt's circumstances could trade as a painter. Instead, Hendrickje and Titus became his employers. With Titus's help Hendrickje, Rembrandt's former maid, opened an art shop where she sold Rembrandt's paintings. Rembrandt was spurred to work harder to meet monetary needs as creditors pressured him to produce paintings in return for loans. The bankruptcy must have been a devastating blow, but there is no direct account of what kind of personal effect the bankruptcy had on Rembrandt who continued to live 13 years after the event.

Individuals unable to meet their financial commitments are forced to juggle between a rock and a hard place in struggling, on one the hand, to pay overdue debts and, on the other, to save money for basic needs. Besides meeting the creditor's requirements, the indebted individuals must pay for food, clothes, and transportation and sustain a place to live – on a daily basis. They have to fight serious deficits under varying institutional conditions, including legal statutes, creditor practices and existing – or non-existing – social security nets (Poppe 2008, p. 11). Coping with debts is a desperate struggle taking its toll on various arenas. Payment default makes the situation even worse as it forces the debtor to deal with the court proceedings described in the previous chapters.

OVER-INDEBTEDNESS AND SOCIO-ECONOMIC POSITION

There is a rich literature on the relationship between socio-economic position (SEP) and various social ills, most notably bad health. Debt and over-indebtedness have a complex and context-bound relationship with SEP. Socio-economic position and its measures refer to an individual's resource, psychosocial, knowledge or prestige-based location within the complex structure of society (Lynch and Kaplan 2000). Also, a number of additional variables or combinations of variables – including wealth, labour market status and race/ethnicity – have been used as proxies of societal status. Income is the most often used measure of SEP, and may still convey relevant short-term information on the connection between material resources and well-being. For a long time, it has been recognized that wealth could be a more meaningful and predictive indicator of material well-being than income, especially for older persons (Henretta and Campbell 1978). Wealth reflects lifetime accumulation of financial resources, while income is a flow and, as such, it is unable to capture long-term financial conditions which constitute the exposure of SEP to various outcome measures (see Cuesta and Budría 2015). As a measure of SEP over-indebtedness captures both income and wealth dimensions. In addition, over-indebtedness has an important psycho-social dimension.

Socio-economic position is a key determinant of health and well-being. One example of numerous studies showing a negative association between low socio-economic position and health is a multi-cohort and meta-analysis study by Stringhini et al. (2017) which demonstrated that, after controlling for known risk factors for non-communicable diseases (harmful use of alcohol, insufficient physical activity, current tobacco use, raised blood pressure, intake of salt or sodium, diabetes and obesity) the participants with low socio-economic status (SES) had greater mortality compared with those with high SES (hazard ratio 1.26, 95 per cent CI 1.21–1.32).

However, it can be argued that the mainstream social epidemiological research has somewhat ignored the fact that the relevance of socio-economic position is undermined by a number of flaws, often related to differences in life-stages, marital status, gender, wealth and so on. For example, income does not necessarily measure real purchasing power when people have major assets or inherited wealth. Similarly, occupational measures are context specific and outdated for the retired population. Lastly, the education-based measures of socio-economic position are usually incomplete due to structural differences in education across time and space (Grundy and Holt 2001). It can be questioned whether traditional measures of socio-economic position really capture efficiently the whole range of stress-, social- and resource-based factors between certain segments of society.

Debt may provide additional information over and above these traditional measures (Drentea and Reynolds 2012). Various side-effects of unmanageable debt, such as home foreclosure, can seriously damage material well-being, which is not reflected in wealth and income-based measures. Debt payment problems may also indirectly affect material well-being by, for example, restricting employment opportunities. Moreover, debt problems may provide additional information about stress-related dimensions of socio-economic position. Debt may also be considered as a psycho-social based measure of socio-economic status. In particular, over-indebtedness entails living under strong financial strain causing psychological stress (Bridges and Disney 2010). This may especially be the case for people outside the labour market whose opportunities to increase income and to pay back debts are constrained.

OVER-INDEBTEDNESS AND POVERTY

Poverty is directly linked to debt since, by definition, poor people have a pervasive need for credit (Townsend 1979). Despite the fact that poverty and over-indebtedness are closely intertwined, it would be a mistake to equate over-indebtedness with small incomes or poverty. As opposed to income level or poverty status, over-indebtedness is a process, where the starting point, as vague as it might be for those living with persistent poverty, is a situation where non-payment is not established. The transition and the qualitative worsening in financial conditions as a result of over-indebtedness may come with social decline.

As far as over-indebtedness relates to relative poverty, it reduces an individual's chances to participate in the minimum acceptable normal way of life. This notion carries numerous dimensions, from access to media to daily diet. Defining poverty through participation in the normal way of life owes much to poverty researcher Peter Townsend, according to whom:

> Individuals, families and groups in the population can be said to be in poverty when they lack the resources to obtain the type of diet, participate in the activities and have the living conditions and amenities which are customary, or at least widely encouraged, or approved, in the societies to which they belong. (Townsend 1979, p. 31)

Poverty means lacking the resources needed to participate in the normal way of life of the surrounding society. However, participation is a broader concept than consumption. It also entails the opportunities and constraints which individuals and households face due to debt problems. Here, Amartya Sen's (1992, p. 110) capability approach to poverty comes in handy: "Poverty is not a matter of low well-being, but the inability to pursue well-being precisely because of the lack of economic means." This opens up the whole poverty discourse to deal with much wider issues than just the scarcity of money (Hiilamo and Kangas 2013). Education, health, cultural and social capital and so on must also be included in the bundle of capabilities needed for the full and free participation in societal activities. Then and only then can we agree that all human beings are equal, that they have certain unalienable rights and that among these are life, liberty and the pursuit of happiness. Over-indebtedness is the inability to pursue well-being as a result of debts.

The European Union (EU) defines at risk of poverty as "individuals or families whose resources are so small as to exclude them from the minimal acceptable way of life of the Member State in which they live" (Atkinson et al. 2002, p. 192). As expressed vividly in this definition, when it comes to poverty the threshold is set against the resources in the population where people live. In defining over-indebtedness, we are operating on an individual level and observing the change accompanied with payment default. In poverty research, we need to determine the minimal acceptable resources for food, clothing, shelter, health care, education and employment. For the study of social consequences of over-indebtedness, we are interested in how these resources are affected by payment default.

There is a multitude of literature on social consequences of relative poverty. Despite the fact that the connection between over-indebtedness and poverty is straightforward, there is very little research focusing on the particular type of relative poverty emerging from over-indebtedness. We do not know, for example, if the constrained resources among over-indebted individuals affect their propensity to vote or to participate in civil society activities. This type of research would be most welcome given the fact that debt discharge policies sometimes regulate very closely the available means, for example, among those going through debt settlement process.

CAUSATIONAL MECHANISMS

The debt-related psycho-social dimension concerns stress. As will be demonstrated below, over-indebtedness is often accompanied by shame, fear of social stigma, anxiety and various forms of psychological distress. Debt can harm human relations by causing strain between the debtor and sureties or by causing intra-family conflict regarding inheritance issues. Over-indebtedness may also be associated with not being able to consume health-enhancing food and services, to access health care and to fully participate in social life (Goode 2012b). In addition, over-indebtedness affects creditworthiness and makes it more difficult to rent an apartment, to make other financial agreements or to find employment (European Commission 2008a).

We may identify two interlinked mechanisms affecting the daily lives of default-debtors, both of which also have societal consequences. The first mechanism is attached to economic constraints caused by over-indebtedness, while the second is connected to stigma of over-indebtedness. Stigma relates to attitudes and behaviours which attest to the psycho-social dimension of over-indebtedness.

The first mechanism, the financial dimension of over-indebtedness concerns lack of necessary resources. It relates to low SEP as a result of over-indebtedness. By definition over-indebtedness is connected with low incomes and negative assets over a long period of time. Lack of money and property have serious consequences across a wide range of social and health outcomes, which will be discussed below.

The second mechanism concerns emotions. Among wealthier countries, the causal link between, for example, indebtedness and health may also run through a mental process where indebted individuals suffer emotions of shame and failure. These emotions, also referred to as financial strain (or worry or concern), may weaken mental health and lead to coping behaviour that is detrimental to health and other social outcomes.

The social stigma concerning indebtedness and debt problems can be analysed from *two perspectives*: firstly, as an internalized psychological condition relating to incidence of over-indebtedness; and, secondly, as related to other people's reactions towards an over-indebted person. The perspectives can be also called subjective and objective dimensions, that is, how people perceive themselves as default-debtors and how other people treat default-debtors.

The concept of moral stressor is important for the first perspective. A moral stressor occurs when "one knows the right thing to do, but institutional constraints make it nearly impossible to pursue the right course of action" (Jameton 1984, p. 6) and persons are unable to fulfil their moral obligations. Default-debtors may feel shame, guilt and embarrassment as a result of failing to meet financial commitments. Social stigma as an internalized psychological condition may perpetuate debt problems due to the fact that it acts as a disincentive to over-indebted consumers seeking relief.

The second dimension of social stigma is related to social norms (Cuesta and Budría 2015). Other people may discriminate against and ostracize over-indebted individuals for neglecting the repayment norm. The respondents in a large EU study revealed feeling humiliated, with negative effects on self-esteem and self-confidence, if they could not conceal their debt problems (CPEC 2013, p. 169). The respondents described social stigma being explicitly externally reinforced with neighbours shunning those who were over-indebted, especially in rural areas.

Earlier research has demonstrated that social stigma is a central element of many default-debtors' everyday lives. Debtors suffer from pervasive and profound feelings of guilt, shame and stigma (Ford 1988; Poppe 2008; CPEC 2013). Severe economic problems lead to changes in social status and reputation, which further aggravate these negative emotions. By analysing interviews of 40 households with mortgage arrears in the UK, Ford (1988, p. 119) showed that default generated strong feeling among the concerned, ranging from anxiety through physical illness to fear. Coping with debts before default had been tiresome, relentless and wearying. Among other things the debtors were concerned about the expected and actual response of those around them, including kin, friends and creditors. The emotional constraints of social stigma may also create moral hazards, leading indebted consumers to ignore market and legal norms.

If and when we take social stigma seriously, we also need to consider the changes in the social contexts. Consequently, we need to acknowledge that attitudes towards debtors may have changed over the years. Efrat (2006) studied the content of newspaper articles on personal bankruptcy published between 1864 and 2002 in the US, and concluded that public perception of bankruptcy had became less stigmatizing since the beginning of the 1960s.

In the event of economic crises, the role of social stigma should lose importance since a large portion of the population is affected by the crises and debt problems become more prevalent. Cuesta and Budría (2015) approach this effect from an individual perspective, claiming that "even though financial burdens hurt, people may feel relatively better once they know that a large part of the population are also affected by financial strain and debts". If many people are hit by debt problems, the over-indebted individuals are less likely to encounter discrimination and ostracization from others. Analysing survey data from Spain, Cuesta and Budría demonstrate a mild social norm effect according to which being less indebted than the reference group resulted, *ceteris paribus,* in better health.

However, in a large EU study, the over-indebted individuals made frequent references to "shame" and described isolating themselves and not letting others know about their problems (CPEC 2013, p. 16). In cases where the household's economic position had previously been higher, the people felt "downgraded". One interviewee referred to being "ashamed" of her situation to the degree she tried to avoid being seen in public: "At one stage, I was almost agoraphobic … I was not leaving the house anymore. I went only out to get food and to collect my children at school" (CPEC 2013, p. 177). A German respondent described her financial difficulties as a "personal defeat".

Loss of socio-economic status may well be a traumatic event. Over-indebted consumers are compelled to give up status-related goods and services, including a chosen living environment with schools, parks and so on. As a working hypothesis, we may assume that the stigma is stronger if over-indebtedness is associated with social decline. It is also important to note that the social stigma of debt is the specific mechanism for over-indebtedness outcomes vis-à-vis social risks which do not carry a social stigma, such as sickness or old age.

Both mechanisms of over-indebtedness, constrained resources and social stigma, operate simultaneously. When it comes to particular outcomes we cannot disentangle their respective effects. This is aptly demonstrated by Desmond (2016, p. 257), who writes about the connection between material and psychological conditions among those who have lost their housing due to unpaid rent: "Substandard housing was a blow to your psychological health: not only because things like dampness, mold, and overcrowding could bring about depression but also because of what living in awful conditions told you about yourself."

The distinction between constrained material resources and social stigma is, however, useful for both theoretical and analytical purposes. We may envision an over-indebted individual feeling no shame about his or her condition and having no negative reactions in the environment (perhaps nobody else knows about the unpaid debts) but suffering terribly from constrained economic resources. Similarly, we can imagine another individual who has, after default, acquired great financial resources (perhaps a successful start-up company or a lottery win) but still suffers from the stigma of once being over-indebted. In the following we will discuss the consequences of over-indebtedness separate from the consequences of limited material resources and as a consequence of social stigma.

Previous literature on the consequences of over-indebtedness has been mostly conducted in social-epidemiology and economics. As most of the available registers and surveys used to study socio-economic status and various measures of well-being do not include a measure of debts, researchers have struggled to find applicable data sources. It is important to note that there are some conflicting dimensions of debt as a determinant of poor socio-economic status (Berger and Houle 2016). Normal and manageable debt may, in fact, have a positive effect on an individual's welfare and health because of increased consumption power. Nevertheless, when debt becomes unmanageable due to, for example, a sudden drop in repayment ability, it may have severe psychological, social and economic consequences. Therefore, the definition of over-indebtedness is of crucial importance for the interpretation of results.

As opposed to the previous chapter, here we will first analyse the consequences of over-indebtedness on an individual level. This is due to the fact that the great majority of the literature discusses individual consequences, and also due to the fact that the focus of this book is on over-indebtedness as a social risk. We start with social participation, and then proceed to financial exclusion, welfare dependence and education as consequences linked to low incomes and assets (Table 4.1). Next, we turn to mental and physical health, employment, human relations and intergenerational effects as outcomes related to stigma of debt. On a societal level, we connect over-indebtedness in terms of incomes and assets with economic growth, the financial industry and housing markets, while general trust, innovation potential and public expenditures are discussed from the perspective of social stigma.

Table 4.1 Individual and societal consequences of over-indebtedness by lack of material resources and stigma of debt

	Individual	Societal
Effect of low incomes and assets	Social participation Financial exclusion Welfare dependence Education	Economic growth Financial industry Housing markets
Effect of debt-related stigma	Mental and physical health Employment Human relations Intergenerational effects	General trust Innovation potential Public expenditures

EFFECTS OF LOW INCOMES AND ASSETS: INDIVIDUAL CONSEQUENCES

Social Participation

Over-indebtedness is not "merely paring back expenses or cutting back on luxuries, such as for example, reducing the number of holidays taken or the frequency of eating out at restaurants" (CPEC 2013, p. 176). The fact that over-indebted individuals have low incomes, and in most cases no assets (or negative assets), means that they have to cut down on all non-essential items. Caplovitz (1979, pp. 94–97) found that his inform-ants suffering the consequences of inflation were first compelled to save money on social activities, which can be described as luxuries, including entertainment, eating out and vacations. However, as problems accumu-lated the households were also forced to give up more necessary items. The non-essential items include social gatherings, meeting friends infor-mally, sporting activities and trips to the cinema (CPEC 2013, p. 178).

Over-indebtedness comes with concrete deterioration of material con-ditions. Households live in fear of a utility or service such as gas, electricity, heating, water or telecommunications being disconnected (CPEC 2013, pp. 185–186). If social participation is seriously limited over-indebted individuals are disconnected from "the larger world" and confined to their homes. Of course, psycho-social processes connected with social stigma of debt may also contribute to the process. Also, Ford (1988, p. 134) reported from her interviews with 40 mortgage defaulters that individuals no longer had drinks in the pub, followed football games, went on family holidays or sent kids on school trips. Credit also allows families to discharge ceremonial and festive commitments such as "appropriately" staged weddings and adequate Christmas celebrations which are respected within their communities (Ford 1988, pp. 188–189). These possibilities are not available to over-indebted families, which may further constrain social participation.

It is evident that the over-indebted situation can be characterized as enforced deprivation – that is, not being able to participate due to lack of funds in the things generally considered the norm in society at a given point in time. Relative deprivation is a result of going without basic necessities as a consequence of inadequate disposable income after the repayment of debts. This is perhaps nothing new for people who have lived their whole lives in poverty. However, a large share of over-indebted individuals come, especially during economic crises, from the middle classes or lower-middle classes which are not used to living with compounded financial restrictions and have to adjust their standards of living to the new reality of over-indebtedness. Eventually the lack of financial means may lead to a downward spiral in social life or a determined withdrawal from social contacts, including evading creditors. The disempowerment and social exclusion accompanied with over-indebtedness will completely prevent participation in normal social activities.

Furthermore, the time and effort needed to get along with limited financial resources may constrain social participation in the normally accepted way of life (see Townsend 1979). As indicated in CPEC (2013) consumer interviews, many over-indebted households struggle to find funds for essential needs, such as food or health care. Over-indebted individuals simply have difficulty making ends meet. They describe their life as a struggle to keep their heads above the water financially, or that they "exist" as opposed to "live". In practical terms, this means that the cupboard is empty and the son goes hungry; the teeth decay with no money to see a dentist. One is not able to afford food needed to keep diabetes under control. One has no money to cover basic school costs or to buy a newspaper. Over-indebted individuals also need to juggle creditors around by "robbing Peter to pay Paul" (Ford 1988, pp. 109–111).

The qualitative worsening of financial situations following the onset of over-indebtedness will also hurt households that are no strangers to poverty. For these households, over-indebtedness could mean, for example, losing a home. Tenants who are unable to pay rent and fall behind in payments may have to accept unpleasant and sometimes dangerous housing conditions or face the risk of eviction and homelessness (Desmond 2016, p. 76). Desmond (2016, p. 98) describes how evictions are shaping the lives of poor black women in the US: "If incarceration had come to define the lives of men from impoverished black neighbourhoods, eviction was shaping the lives of women. Poor black men were locked up. Poor black women were locked out."

Financial Exclusion

The status as over-indebted signifies that the individual is not able to access financial services available to other people with a good credit history. The European Commission (2008b, p. 9) defines financial exclusion as "a process whereby people encounter difficulties accessing and/or using financial services and products in the mainstream market that are appropriate to their needs and enable them to lead a normal social life in the society in which they belong". In practical terms this means that the individuals are unable to take on new credit even if the person involved is willing to pay a higher level of interest, or that they need to seek credit from unregulated or usurious lenders, sometimes described as "doorstep lenders" or "moneylenders" (CPEC 2013, p. 187).

In addition to credit exclusion banking exclusion is another key aspect of financial exclusion. Depending on national legislation, over-indebted persons may experience the freezing or a closure of a current account, or they may lack access to a debit card or to a cheque book. In Germany and the UK, for example, a bad credit history can be used to prevent people from opening a bank account, while in Finland, Norway and the Netherlands, it is not possible to do so (CPEC 2013, p. 188).

A Federal Deposit Insurance Corporation (FDIC) survey showed that 7 per cent of US households were "unbanked", meaning that no one in the household had a checking or savings account, while an additional 19.9 per cent of households were "underbanked", meaning that the household had an account at an insured institution but also obtained financial services and products outside of the banking system (FDIC 2016). The main reason for being unbanked given by the respondents was that they did not have enough money to keep in an account.

Welfare Dependence

Lack of financial means due to over-indebtedness leads individuals to seek whatever financial assistance is available for them to cover their daily expenses. That includes both public and private sources of social assistance, which is delivered, for example, in cash benefits and benefits in kind. They need assistance not only to cover their daily expenses but also to help pay remaining overdue debts. If they have lost their primary residence, they may need to rely on rental or social housing. Bad credit history is an obstacle to renting an apartment, which may further increase the need for public housing assistance.

As a result of over-indebtedness households are also excluded from a number of services. It is difficult for them, for example, to take out a phone or internet subscription, get an insurance policy or find a job (CPEC 2013, p. 189; Ford 1988, p. 137). When a property or life insurance policy is terminated the household faces more risks in the future. These consequences of over-indebtedness tend to increase the need for public assistance. With very few exceptions the legislated minimum income schemes offer no help to pay off debts. The same goes for charitable financial help. This means that over-indebted households are likely to be dependent on welfare for a long time. Welfare dependency comes with poor work incentives since extra incomes are, in many cases, deducted from benefits.

Education

Over-indebtedness may weaken individuals' chances for human capital investments. That is especially the case where institutions of higher education charge high tuition fees. Unpaid fees prevent graduation. Also in countries with free education, payment default entry may prevent a student from getting a study loan. To our knowledge no quantitative study has particularly focused on the effect of over-indebtedness on educational outcomes. However, a study from Finland showed that debt problems are associated with dropping out of secondary education (Majamaa et al. 2017).

With poverty status as a measure, Crosnoe et al. used the family process model to study the link between early economic disadvantage and later enrolment in higher education in the US. Data was employed from the Philadelphia project on successful adolescent development in a high-risk setting. The results suggest that economically disadvantaged parents are less optimistic about their adolescents' educational opportunities. In response, they engage less in the proactive parenting that encourages enrolment. The researchers concluded that "this lack of hope can be self-fulfilling, interfering with positive parenting in ways that negatively affect the adolescent's transition to adulthood" (Crosnoe et al. 2002, p. 700). However, parents can substitute the economic disadvantage with non-economic support, including ensuring their adolescents are in a protective environment and mapping out opportunities for them.

LOW INCOMES AND ASSETS: SOCIETAL CONSEQUENCES

Economic growth

Over-indebtedness has negative consequences also on the societal level. Recent research has convincingly demonstrated a negative loop of over-indebtedness and economic recessions (Mian and Sufi 2015a). If households are heavily indebted before recession, they are extremely vulnerable to negative changes in incomes, asset prices and cost of debt. When a shock occurs, for example as a result of unemployment or decrease in housing prices, the households cut spending, which will decrease overall demand in the economy. In turn, that will exacerbate unemployment. Worsening economic conditions again add pressure on government finances, which can lead to further income shocks in the form of austerity measures such as social welfare cuts and higher taxes (CPEC 2013,

p. 198). That will push more households into over-indebtedness, further increasing the effects of the recession. This development will create a negative feedback loop where reduced domestic demand for products and services means less employment and lower incomes.

Empirical research has convincingly demonstrated that high levels of pre-bust household debt to income cause deeper falls in consumption and employment compared to recessions preceded by low levels of pre-bust debt to income (Mian and Sufi 2015a; CPEC 2013). Mian and Sufi (2015a, p. 43) point out that the bursting of the investor-led tech bubble in the early 2000s did not result in economic contraction, while the bursting of the housing bubble in 2007 caused deep economic crises.

Igan et al. (2012) found that in a sample of 99 housing busts and recessions among 25 rich countries from 1980 to 2011 large increases in household debt to income ratios before the crises were associated with significantly larger contractions in economic activity. In addition, the study observed that household deleveraging (that is, a decrease in the debt to income ratio) was more pronounced following busts preceded by a larger run-up in household debt. The fact that a larger accumulation of household debt was followed by deeper and more prolonged downturns indicates that the results are not simply a reflection of banking crises, but that higher debt to income ratios independently cause worse contractions in economic activity when house prices and growth fall. Earlier literature has also shown that recessions preceded by economy-wide credit booms tend to be deeper and more protracted than other recessions (Terrones et al. 2011) and that consumption volatility is positively correlated with household debt (Isaksen et al. 2011).

With data from 238 counties with more than 100 000 residents across the US, Mian and Sufi (2011) analysed the association of household debt and employment in the US. The results provided more evidence for the negative loop of over-indebtedness and economic recessions by showing a close negative link between employment and household debt. Counties with high household debt experienced relatively high employment declines well before the recession began. During the most severe part of the recession, employment losses in high household debt counties were dramatic. Total employment declined by 7 per cent from the second quarter of 2008 to the second quarter of 2009. Furthermore, employment remained at extremely depressed levels in high household debt counties through the second quarter of 2010. By contrast, employment growth in low household debt counties stabilized as early as the second quarter of 2009. Total job losses were much lower. The results indicate that high household debt leads to lower consumption, which brings about the lower production of goods, which turns into reduced employment.

The International Monetary Fund (IMF) concluded in the 2012 World Economic Outlook that recession triggered by household debt could result in slower recovery than those triggered by other events. According to the IMF, prevention of foreclosures and writing off household debts were needed to support economic growth. Also, the Great Depression in the 1930s was preceded by a large run-up in household debt (Mian and Sufi 2015a, p. 5).

The theoretical point of the literature described above is that when a shock hits the borrowing capacity of debtors with a high marginal propensity to consume it forces them to reduce their debt. In turn, that will then lead to a decline in aggregate economic activity. Also, the increased uncertainty can give a reason for precautionary saving, which would further depress consumption. Mian and Sufi (2015a, p. 9) conclude confidently that *"economic disasters are almost always preceded by a large increase in household debt"* (emphasis in original).

Financial Industry

Over-indebtedness comes with other structural economic consequences besides negative impact on economic growth. When negative income or wealth shock occurs, creditors are also hurt. The debtors will have difficulties meeting their commitments. That will cause an increase in non-performing loans and weaken bank balances, especially if the households were heavily indebted before the crisis. This will lead to more restricted access to credit, as financial institutions become more cautious in lending, and reduce economic output. That was the case, for example, in Finland in the early 1990s during the deep economic recession, which was also characterized by the bursting of the housing bubble (Kiander and Vartia 2011).

Credit crunch is the first effect of large-scale debt problems for financial institutions. A rise in non-performing loans makes the institutions wary of lending. They lose potential customers in order to decrease risks. When a number of financial institutions risk default the stability of the whole financial system is reduced with a contagious effect among other banks. Over-indebtedness does not hurt banks and other lenders only through increase in non-performing loans. With high prevalence of over-indebtedness the asset prices (for example housing) also tend to fall, which will further weaken balance sheets. If creditors repossess and carry out fire sales en masse, their own assets also lose value. This may lead to a decrease in trust of financial institutions, banking crises and disruption of domestic or international financial systems (Mian and Sufi 2015a).

The Global economic crises and the following banking crises in Europe witnessed massive credit write-downs, bank insolvencies and effective nationalization of some of the major banks. The colossal bail-outs ruined the reputation of financial institutions and led to a temporary surge in banking regulation (van Cruijsen et al. 2016). That effect was short-lived, but it may be reflected in the general lack of trust in society and politicians and ensuing support for populism (we will return to this topic later).

Housing Markets

The most dramatic effect of over-indebtedness on housing is seen in the negative externalities associated with foreclosures and fire sales (Mian and Sufi 2015a, pp. 27–28). Using data from the US state of Massachusetts, Campbell et al. (2011) suggest that a single foreclosure lowers the price of a neighbouring property by about 1 per cent. Interestingly, the effects can be much larger when there is a wave of foreclosures, with estimates of price declines reaching almost 30 per cent. Reduced housing prices send negative signals of economic activity through a number of self-reinforcing contractionary spirals, including negative wealth effects, a reduction in collateral value, a negative impact on bank balances and credit crunch.

Losing a home may be the most dramatic immediate consequence of over-indebtedness on an individual level. On the societal level, over-indebtedness can lead to a general weakening of housing standards. With decreasing prices, there are not enough investments in building new homes and renovating old ones. The households need to settle for substandard housing. General housing standards may also deteriorate as a result of indebted homeowners' behaviour. Homeowners at risk of default reduce investments in their property in expectation that some value will go to the lender in the event of foreclosure (Melzer 2017). With foreclosure approaching, homeowners lack the incentive to undertake even basic, economically efficient repairs, such as fixing a roof or plumbing a leak.

EFFECTS OF DEBT-RELATED STIGMA: INDIVIDUAL CONSEQUENCES

Mental health

The bulk of research focusing on consequences of over-indebtedness is concentrated on health, especially mental health. The association between debt and mental health is well established. The link goes through debt-related stigma. Already Caplovitz (1974) showed that a number of default-debtors suffered from stress-related symptoms such as tension, headaches, insomnia, upset stomach and loss of appetite. A similar picture emerged from a large-scale interview study in Europe which lists a large number of self-reported impacts under both psychological and well-being impacts related to the onset of debt problems and physical manifestations related to the onset of debt problems (CPEC 2013, p. 181) (Table 4.2).

A few systematic reviews exist regarding the relationship between debt and health. A systematic review and meta-analysis by Richardson et al. (2013) demonstrated a strong relationship between unsecured debt and health, especially between debt and mental health, in particular depression. The majority of the previous studies utilized limited cross-sectional and retrospective data.

The summary produced by Turunen and Hiilamo (2014) showed that the onset of mortgage indebtedness was associated with deteriorating mental health, and persons who failed to pay their mortgage or whose house was repossessed reported a particularly high prevalence of mental and physical health impairments. They experienced poorer health relative to homeowners with no housing strain for every measure examined, including the number of days in the past month that mental health was impaired (other measures include self-rated health, psychological distress, the number of days in the past month that physical health was impaired and physical symptoms). McLaughlin et al. (2012) also found foreclosure to be associated with an increased rate of symptoms pertaining to major depression and generalized anxiety disorder.

Poor health-related behaviour, work disability due to mental illness and overall depression are significantly higher for persons with some form of debt or debt-related problems (Richardson et al. 2013). A study focusing on older US populations suggests that dichotomous debt status can be individually and strongly associated with depression over and above conventional measures of socio-economic position (Drentea and Reynolds 2012).

So far most of the research on health effects of over-indebtedness is coming from market model personal insolvency countries, namely the US and the UK. In the review by Turunen and Hiilamo (2014) almost half of the reviews (33 studies) were focusing on the US, while a third focused on the UK. The results reflect the national context. For example, Alley et al. (2011) showed that mortgage delinquency and defaulting on a housing loan (borrower had given a lien on the property as collateral for the loan) among Americans older than 50 years were associated with a significant elevation in the incidence of depressive symptoms, food insecurity and cost-related medication non-adherence. The first observation is almost universal, but the second and the third are most likely related to a US-specific context.

Table 4.2   Reported impacts of over-indebtedness by EU households (N=120)

Type	Self-reported impacts
Psychological and well-being impacts related to the onset of debt problems	Depression (multiple responses) Stress (multiple responses) Pressure (constant) Worry (continual) Feeling "worn out" Fragility/anguish/anxiety Needing "calm and rest" Being scared/living in fear Being alone – having time to think Frustration Nervousness Helplessness/despair/hopelessness Vulnerability Loss of control Feeling of "betrayal" Guilt Feeling "discouraged"
Physical manifestations related to the onset of debt problems	Sleep deprivation (multiple responses) Medication/treatments/antidepressants (multiple responses) Crying Vomiting Increased alcohol consumption Ulcers Weight loss/weight gain (comfort eating)/hunger Circulatory problems Physical appearance (looking worse) Seeking professional help (doctor, psychiatrist, therapist) Admission to hospital Self-harm Obsessive-compulsive disorder (OCD) Panic attacks Stomach aches Burnout Asthma/shortage of breath Suicidal ideation (Note: in some cases, existing conditions were reported to have deteriorated)

Source: CPEC (2013, p. 181).

Suicide

Richardson et al. (2013) found that those with debt had odds of 3.24 of mental disorder, 2.77 of depression and 7.9 of completed suicide. A systematic review by Turunen and Hiilamo (2014) showed that individuals with unmet loan payments had suicidal ideation and suffered from depression more often than those without such financial problems. Unpaid financial obligations were also related to poorer subjective health and health-related behaviour. Some studies have pointed out that over-indebted gamblers have a particularly high risk of suicide (Blaszczynski and Farrell 1998; Wong et al. 2010).

Kidger et al. (2011) found that individuals admitted to a trauma centre following an attempted suicide in the US were more than twice as likely to become bankrupt within two years compared to those who were admitted following an accident. The relationship between attempted suicide and pre-injury bankruptcy was weaker but still visible, particularly when bankruptcy was restricted to Chapter 7 (in US bankruptcy law) liquidation cases.

Lenton and Mosley (2008) showed that a high-interest debt repayment structure and worry exacerbate debt problems and influence health-seeking behaviour in the UK. Studies from Germany show that indebtedness and unemployment correlate slightly with mortality (Brzoska and Razum 2008) and with suicide rates (Weyerer and Wiedenmann 1995). In a similar vein, a study from Australia showed that financial stress is higher in families with more children, with more income units and dependants and with an older head of the household as well as among families from ethnic minorities (Worthington 2006).

There is also some research on protective factors. Selenko and Batinic (2011) showed that financial strain had less effect on mental health if the individual had strong self-efficacy beliefs, a belief in his or her own competence, a belief in his or her ability to cope, and greater access to some sort of collective purpose. In addition, having more access to social contacts was related to better mental health. That was the case, however, only if the perceived financial strain was low.

Mechanisms linking over-indebtedness to mental health

It is still not clear what the causal mechanisms are linking over-indebtedness to mental health problems. The most likely candidates are physiological and behavioural consequences of chronic stress. It is assumed that psycho-social factors are the pathway through which low socio-economic status "gets under the skin". Despite a substantial body of literature, the exact mechanism for this pathway is not yet fully understood. Earlier research has established that dysregulation of basal cortisol rhythms, elevations in blood pressure and inflammatory markers, and metabolic alterations associated with health behaviours are all linked to chronic stress exposure and are important indicators of disease susceptibility (McEwen 1998, 2004). Exploring the association of these biomarkers with debt would provide valuable information on the pathways through which debt becomes embodied (Sweet et al. 2013). The stigma of debt can also affect health behaviour; for example, it can restrict participation in health promoting social activities or, alternatively, lead to unhealthy behaviour such as smoking, heavy drinking and drug use. The lack of financial resources, the first dimension of over-indebtedness, may limit access to health resources. Garcia and Draut (2009) found that in the US one-third of indebted households have given up medical care in order reduce family expenses.

The connections between indebtedness and poor health are not clear-cut. Instead, they are influenced by factors such as source of debt, collateral status, repayment structure and interest rates. Employment status, the value of assets and personality traits act as mediating factors (Turunen and Hiilamo 2014). In addition, as we argue in this book, the debt collection and personal insolvency regimes may play a role.

Despite a strong association between debt and mental health it is still arguable whether overdue debts actually *cause* poor mental health (for discussion, see Cuesta and Budría 2015). The causation of indebtedness and mental health is likely to run in two directions. Debt can lead to bad health, just as bad health can result in debt. Inverse causation is possible when prior problems in mental health cause an exit from paid employment which, in turn, leads to debt problems due to decrease in repayment possibilities.

Using individual-level UK panel data and local house price movements exogenous to individual households, Gathergood (2012b) found that individuals with debt repaying problems in localities with a higher bankruptcy rate experienced less deterioration of their mental well-being. Using three waves of Spanish Survey of Household Finances, Cuesta and Budría (2015) showed that non-mortgage debt payments and debt arrears significantly affect people's health. With regard to social stigma, they demonstrated that being less indebted than the reference group results, *ceteris paribus,* in better health. These studies pay attention to the easily ignored fact that general economic conditions may play a role in the connection between indebtedness and health. Large-scale economic shock affecting a large portion of the population may carry less of a social burden for indebted individuals than experiencing such problems during an economic upswing (see also Klein 2016). The results speak for the importance of social stigma in consequences of over-indebtedness.

Establishing the causal effect is very difficult since experimental social studies are not ethically acceptable. The lack of longitudinal studies and weaknesses in the exiting studies makes it difficult to demonstrate causality. In a study by Meltzer et al. (2013), there was no multiplicative effect of debt and addictive behaviours, so it looks as though addictive behaviours have an effect on common mental disorders apart from debt. Using fixed effect models with the German Socio-economic Panel data, Keese and Schmitz (2014) suggest moderate effects of debt (consumer credit and mortgage) on health, which are qualitatively the same for two distinct debt measures, consumer credit and home loans. Other studies have utilized instrumental variables to circumvent endogeneity problems. The results are somewhat mixed but point towards causality from debt to health (for example Gathergood 2012b).

In assessing and comparing earlier evidence it needs to be taken into account that these studies (and others) have used different measures of over-indebtedness; focused on specific, often non-representative, populations; analysed effects of different types of debts (mortgage, medical debt, credit card debt, loans from friends or relatives); and utilized heterogeneous and incomparable measures of mental health. The data sources also differ across studies. Consequently, the studies have used diverse sets of variables, including gender, age, race/ethnicity, education, income, marital status, employment status, number of children/family size/household size, health insurance status or Medicaid eligibility and housing status (including homeownership/housing tenure/household tenure) as confounding factors. Two Finnish studies on the association of over-indebtedness with chronic disease and disability retirement actually showed stronger associations for women than for men (Blomgren et al. 2016, 2017). Cuesta and Budría (2015) found that debt to income ratios were slightly more relevant in explaining women's health status than men's, and that the difference was statistically significant.

With regard to methods, previous studies have used panel surveys, nationally representative epidemiological surveys and psychological autopsy studies to examine the relationship. There is a lack of knowledge about cross-country differences in the association between mental health and household indebtedness. Cross-country evidence would be important for recognizing effective policy strategies that ease health consequences of increasing indebtedness.

The studies have used data for general population and specific populations such as university students, debt management clients and older adults. For those in mid and later life, mental health consequences of indebtedness may be particularly severe. In this age group individuals face reduced opportunities to increase income to pay off debts. This may result in greater feelings of shame. In addition, older people may have lower levels of financial literacy. There is also a possibility for inter-generational conflict with potential heirs. Most previous studies of indebtedness and mental health have focused on younger people, apart from a few studies of the US population (for example Drentea and Reynolds 2012; Alley et al 2011). In the European context, little is known about specific consequences of debt in the older population, which emphasizes the need for more research.

Physical health

Mental and physical health are closely connected. For example, depression associated with financial problems may worsen physical health, while back pain associated with financial problems can lead to depression. A number of studies have simultaneously analysed both mental and physical health outcomes.

The mechanism linking debts to physical health include both stress- and health-related behaviour. A cross-sectional survey among clients of officially approved debt and insolvency counselling centres in Germany identified over-indebted individuals, and particularly over-indebted men, as a high-risk group of smokers (Rueger et al. 2013). Those with low levels of social embeddedness or support were especially likely to increase smoking after becoming over-indebted.

In a study on US college students' credit card debt (above 1000 dollars), it was found to be a more robust indicator of unhealthy weight-related behaviours compared to either high perceived stress or poor stress management, which were not statistically significant (Nelson et al. 2008). Weight-related behaviours included physical (in)activity, sedentary behaviour (such as watching TV), dietary patterns, unhealthy weight-control behaviours and body satisfaction. Credit card debt and poor stress management significantly predicted risk behaviours of engaging in physical fights, binge drinking and using tobacco, marijuana and/or other drugs.

A study by Münster et al. (2009) from Germany found that over-indebtedness was associated with an increased prevalence of over-weight and obesity that was not explained by traditional definitions of socio-economic status. With data from the US, Averett and Smith (2014) demonstrated that women are more likely to be overweight when they have trouble paying bills, while no such effects are observed among men.

In a study by Drentea and Lavrakas (2000), the ratio of credit card debt to total family income among residents of the US state of Ohio was significantly associated with worse physical health and worse self-reported health. Havlik et al. (1992) found that in the US there was a significantly higher occurrence of bankruptcy or unemployment and divorce or marital separation in the five years prior to the clinical presentation of 56 melanoma patients relative to a control group: 20 per cent of melanoma patients had sustained a major financial crisis involving bankruptcy or unemployment prior to clinical presentation. This may relate to increased health care-seeking behaviour or reflect an increased susceptibility of the patient following major psychosocial stress.

Both of the above-mentioned studies were conducted in the US. However, there is emerging evidence on the association between over-indebtedness and physical health also from other countries. Using EU-SILC data, Angel (2016) found that after controlling for both observed and unobserved time-constant heterogeneity, indicators of over-indebtedness based on arrears for different payment obligations increase the likelihood of subjective experience of bad/very bad health, independently of income, education and other dimensions of socio-economic status. However, the effect was only short term and not very strong.

Studies from Finland have shown that over-indebtedness is also associated with incidence of chronic disease, including severe depression, in a follow-up setting and with the risk of disability retirement in all diagnostic groups (Blomgren et al. 2016, 2017). These retrospective epidemiological studies were based on analysis of persons who had over-indebted with recorded credit default entries for at least 15 years. Ochsmann et al. (2009) found that over-indebtedness was strongly associated with back pain in Germany.

Two studies have tried to link the health effects of over-indebtedness to decreased use of health services as a result of unpaid debts. Using EU-SILC data, Angel (2016) studied whether institutional factors (accessibility and private cost of health services, debt management and debt discharge regulations, dispute resolution with banks/insurance companies) were associated with the effect size of over-indebtedness on health. Some evidence was found that higher debt-collection costs are associated with a stronger effect of over-indebtedness on subjectively assessed poor health. However, there was no association between accessibility and private cost of health services and the effect size of over-indebtedness on health. Keese and Schmitz (2014) studying Germany did not find support for the health cost argument. Actually, they showed that members of indebted households were more likely to see a doctor, indicating the fact that private health costs are generally low in most European welfare states.

Employment

In moral terms, one of the worst outcomes of over-indebtedness is that the debtor loses the ability to earn a sufficient income, service the debts and exit over-indebtedness because of social exclusion from the work environment, banking and other financial connections (Haas 2006). Losing a job, or having difficulties finding one, may result both from subjective and objective experience of social stigma. The effects of feeling a failure may undermine a default-debtor's ability to access employment. The lack of self-confidence resulting from over-indebtedness may come across badly at job interviews (including becoming upset during them).

Potential employers may also ostracize applicants with a bad credit history. Potential employers regard, for example, wage attachments as an indicator of an unbalanced way of living. The over-indebted person who hides the truth about his/her current wage attachment in a job interview could be dismissed once the attachment is discovered by the employer. Wage attachments should not, strictly speaking, be a reason for dismissal or a barrier to engagement, but in reality they could be (CPEC 2013, p. 190). With wage attachments or agreed terms of debt settlement there are also built-in disincentives for work. The debtor may not be motivated to earn more if all excess income goes to repay the debts. One over-indebted interviewee in the EU study expressed de-motivation towards work for not knowing that earnings would be required to go towards repaying debts, as opposed to being available for pleasurable activities (CPEC 2013, p. 190).

Status as an over-indebted individual may also affect those who are in work. It could reflect negatively in relationships at work or decrease work productivity. At the acute stage of over-indebtedness workers may have difficulty keeping debt worries out of their minds and concentrating on their work. Over-indebtedness often requires time off work due to stress. They may also need to stay away from work for debt stress-related illnesses. A reason for unwillingness to move into paid work could also be the consequence of feeling a failure, which undermines and demotivates the over-indebted to participate in the labour market (CPEC 2013, p. 189). As a result of discrimination in the labour market, self-employment may be an alternative for the over-indebted. Nonetheless, many start-ups fail.

It is a fact that wage garnishment and seizure remove incentives to work, and there is evidence of unwillingness to work among over-indebted individuals; but the lack of motivation to work should not be exaggerated since the great majority of debtors are available for work. Analysing data from the Families and Children Study (FACS) from 1999 to 2002 in the UK, Kempson et al. (2004) argue that, in general, the rates of movement into work for families with arrears and those without arrears are not significantly different. The fastest rate of return to work was found in families in arrears with credit commitment, while the slowest rate was among families with household bill arrears. Regarding moving out of paid work, overall, families who were in arrears were twice as likely to move out of paid work of 16 or more hours a week. The rate of leaving work among lone parents was slightly higher than that for couples. Seemingly, there were strong links between leaving paid work and arrears on household bills and housing costs. It needs to be taken into account that arrears may be related to health factors such as ill-health and stress which could influence the move out of work.

Human Relations

Relationship satisfaction could be defined as the measurement of a person's feelings, thoughts and behaviours about their marital, or similar intimate, relationship (Hendrick 1988). Literature on family studies often focuses on the impact of partner communication, decision making and conflict negotiations. Very few studies emphasize the linkages between financial behaviours and relationship satisfaction (see Ford 1988, pp. 109–111). Social exchange theory is used to analyse union formation and dissolution. The theory explains that any physical, social or psychological pleasure is regarded as a reward, whereas anything that a person dislikes is classified as an opportunity cost (White and Klein 2002). When the reward exceeds the cost, a profit occurs. On the other hand, cost exceeding the reward results in a loss. When the benefit-to-cost analysis meets or exceeds expectations, individuals remain happy in their relationship. When the benefits are below the expectation, the couple becomes dissatisfied and examines the relationship. If the benefits of alternative solutions outweigh the costs of leaving the relationship, they are likely to dissolve the union (Dew 2007, 2008, 2011).

Research leaves little doubt that stress accompanied by over-indebtedness may interrupt family stability and increase tension between spouses, family members and friends. It is often found that when a household enters a "debt spiral" with no prospect of recovery, severe depression, relationship break-up and other problems are likely to result

(Eurofound 2012). Already Caplovitz (1974, pp. 283–285; 1979, pp. 119–137) argued that economic problems may either strengthen or destroy family spirit. The notion is dependent on the pre-crisis situation. As Poppe (2008, p. 47) argues, happy marriages are of course more resistant to hardships than unhappy ones.

It appears that a small number of studies have paid particular attention to the connection between debt and marriage satisfaction. Dew (2008) considered recently married couples and their marital satisfaction change in relation to debt change. His study suggests that consumer debt represents a challenge for newlyweds as the couples struggle to maintain their levels of marital satisfaction. Consumer debt is a key factor for becoming less satisfied with the marriage, particularly if couples have no prior debt but later assume a great deal. Dew argues that the ways in which consumer debt affects relationship satisfaction are also through various rational mechanisms, including loss of time together, conflict over finances or perceptions of financial unfairness.

Edwards (2003) analysed data from a survey on the experience of debt conducted among clients of the Citizen Advice Bureaux (CABs) in the UK: 18 per cent of the sample stated that they had arguments with their partners, while some faced relationship problems and disagreements within their wider family circle. Respondents with children reported shame about not being able to financially support their children's needs, letting their children be excluded from participating in activities with friends. Many mentioned the lack of social life, having no holidays and that their plan for buying a home had to be put on hold. Similarly, findings from a survey of 1647 households nationwide by the Minister for Employment Relations and Consumer Affairs UK show that, aside from anxiety and stress, lack of money and relationship tensions were the most common consequences of debt, occurring in 1 in 12 households (Kempson 2002).

In Dew's (2011) study in the US on the association between consumer debt and divorce (longitudinal data from 1987–1988 and 1992–1994), consumer debt was negatively associated with both husband's and wife's marital satisfaction. The more consumer debt couples had, the less happy they were in their marriage. Consumer debt, Dew asserted, caused financial disagreements and made individuals feel financially unstable.

On a similar note, Kempson et al. studied the impact of arrears in the UK using the FACS surveys in 1999, 2000, 2001 and 2002. They argue that "arrears are acting in conjunction with sustained financial strain when it is liked to a couple separating" (Kempson et al. 2004, p. 82). The type of arrears and the level of income also play an important role. Couples with children who had any arrears were more likely to separate than couples without children. The highest rate of separation was found in families with arrears on household costs and in families who had fallen behind with payments on household bills (often found in low-income families). Meanwhile, the rate of splitting up was small in families with credit arrears (often found in high-income families).

Interviewees in the Civic Consulting of the Consumer Policy Evaluation Consortium study demonstrated that over-indebtedness could have a contrasting impact on a relationship (CPEC 2013, p. 182). It could bring a couple closer, but more often it could be a source of instability. The respondents described tension, argument or "friction", which was often termed "regular" or "constant". One respondent summed this up by using the phrase "the climate is heavy". The source of strife was, for example, the assignment of blame to the other party for incurring individual debts, for overspending, for not doing enough to increase household income or for doing too much. One respondent reported that "his relationship had deteriorated as a result of him spending more hours at work for the purpose of raising extra income (by way of overtime) for the primary purpose of discharging household debts" (CPEC 2013, p 193).

CPEC's (2013, p. 191) results showed that over-indebtedness may cause relationship strain due to financial difficulty. To be precise, there is the assignment of blame to one partner for causing over-indebtedness. In some families, the relationship deteriorated due to hard work to raise extra money in order to discharge household debts. Further, many parents cannot fund their children's social activities with friends. Due to lack of money, some families with over-indebtedness have to limit their socializing opportunities with friends and family members, which decreases marital satisfaction.

There are debates over whether it is household asset holding or household debt that causes marital instability. Chang and Lee (2006) considered the Korean Labour and Income Panel Study household surveys in 1998 of 5000 randomly selected households. They conclude that there was no significant effect of the size of debt or the debt-to-income ratio on marital instability, but that the household asset holdings or household net worth were the important factors contributing to marital instability. In contrast, Dew (2007) analysed the first two panels of the US National Study of Families and Households (NSFH) to study the roles of assets and consumer debts in marriage. He concluded that assets could reduce feelings of economic pressure but do not directly relate to marriage. However, consumer debt directly relates to marriage as the debt could limit future choices, leading to marital distress.

Interestingly, Vinokur et al. found a connection between financial strain and relationship satisfaction in families with an unemployed partner. Their study investigated how financial strain affects depression and relationship satisfaction of unemployed persons and their spouses. They explain that financial strain can have an impact on depressive symptoms as well as the relationship satisfaction in couples who are facing job loss. Depression can deteriorate social support. Depressive symptoms may diminish a partner's ability to offer support to the job seeker (for example expressing care and concern) and, in the meantime, increase the partner's undermining behaviours (criticizing, insulting). According to Vinokur et al. (1996, p. 175), "the combination of decreased support and increased undermining has two separate effects on the job seeker: it increases depressive symptoms and reduces relationship satisfaction".

The problem of reverse causality also concerns studies of over-indebtedness and divorce. Fisher and Lyons's (2006) study on the relationship between debt, bankruptcy and divorce shows that bankruptcy does not directly affect divorce. However, it is financial difficulty that directly leads either to divorce or to bankruptcy. It is also possible that couple divorce for strategic reasons. In the CPEC (2013, p. 183) study one of the UK respondents explained that he had left the family home in order to allow his partner to receive more social welfare benefits.

Debt can deteriorate the relationship expectations beyond financial security, for instance, less time spent together due to work and employment change. The effects of consumer debt apparently lead to conflict between the married couples. The more conflict they hold, the higher chance of divorce they have. Britt et al. (2008) studied how perceived partner spending behaviours influence relationship satisfaction in the US. The sample consisted of residents from several communities within one Mid-Western state. The results revealed that those who perceived their partner's behaviours negatively were more likely to be dissatisfied. Hence, the perceived negative spending behaviours of the partner could be seen as a cost to respondents, and were thus related to lower relationship satisfaction.

It is important to note that various demographic and socio-economic variables (age, gender, employment status, number of children, race/ethnic background, educational level, homeownership and household income) shape the association between debt and divorce or relationship satisfaction. The effects of debt-related divorce are often more severe for women than for men. Women tend to stay in the same home and take responsibility for joint debts after relationship breakdown, while men move out (Bull 2007).

Over-indebtedness may affect human relationships beyond the intimate partner relationship. Asking for help from better-off family members can be complicated. Asking for irregular loans from friends and acquaintances is not an easy task. With observation data from Milwaukee in the US, Desmond (2016, p. 121) notes:

> Those ties were banked, saved for emergency situations or opportunities to get ahead. People were careful not to overdraw their account because when family members with money grew exhausted by repeated requests, they sometimes withheld support for long periods of time, pegging their relatives' misfortunes to individual failings. This was one reason why family members in the best position to help were often not asked do so.

In the CPEC interview study a respondent from Germany described a dwindling number or withdrawal of friends as socializing became impossible through lack of money. Another German respondent reported her family "turning their backs on her". Yet another German respondent told about a complete loss of contact with her parents as a result of her financial difficulties (CPEC 2013, p. 183). The situation is all the more difficult if relatives or friends have provided security for the debt. If the original debtor defaults the third party may lose property or enter over-indebtedness. The prolonged stressful situation of over-indebtedness may also alter the social identities of those affected (Poppe 2008). They have lost the freedom to use consumption to define their social identities. It could be difficult to find a new role in social life after losing control of financial resources.

Intergenerational Effects

Where, when and to whom you are born largely determines what opportunities you will have in life. In the CPEC (2013, p. 191) study many interviewees were concerned about the effect of over-indebtedness on their children. When a household is under financial stress the parents need to cut down all spending, including spending on their children. This means that the over-indebted cannot, for example, afford to send their children to extracurricular activities and do what their friends and classmates are doing (CPEC 2013, p. 179).

Apart from limited resources, the stigma of debt is also likely to have an effect on children of the over-indebted individuals. Take for example parenting. One respondent in the CPEC (2013, p. 183) study described being short-tempered with his children: "That can affect your children you know, you're playing with them and you start shouting at them. You don't need to shout at them, it's just that you've got other things on your mind." The respondents described it as very hard to ask the children to make sacrifices. That weighed heavily on parents. One German respondent noted: "that ruins you psychologically". Sometimes the effect of debts can be really harsh on children. One respondent was under such serious stress that she sent her daughter to stay with her mother as she could not afford to feed the child.

In the US context Desmond (2016, pp. 240–241) describes a black single mother's struggle to secure housing:

> Arleen sacrificed for her boys, fed them as best as she could, clothed them with what she had. But when they wanted more than she could give, she always had ways, some subtle, others not, of telling them that they didn't deserve it. – You could only say "I'm sorry, I can't" so many time before you began to feel worthless, edging closer to a breaking point. So you protect yourself, in a reflexive way, by finding ways to say "No, I won't." I cannot help you. So, I will find you unworthy of help.

Psychological research generally concludes that economic deprivation is associated with a less nurturing and more punitive and inconsistent child-raising behaviour (Poppe 2008, p. 47). This is explained in terms of the anxiety, irritability and depression that accompany financial difficulties. Studying the impact of economic hardship on black families and children in the US, McLoyd (1990) observed that poverty and economic loss diminish parents' capacity for supportive, consistent and involved parenting, and render parents more vulnerable to the debilitating effects of negative life events. McLoyd identified as a major mediator of the link between economic hardship and parenting behaviour psychological distress deriving from an excess of negative life events, undesirable chronic conditions, and the absence and disruption of marital bonds. A more recent study by Neppl et al. (2016) confirmed in a prospective, longitudinal setting the Family Stress Model (FST) with data from the US state of Iowa. According to the Federal Trade Commission (2017), economic hardship led to economic pressure, which is associated with parental emotional distress and couple conflict, which is again associated with harsh parenting and child problem behaviour.

Children are exposed to the uncertainties following over-indebtedness in the family, including not only the general physical and mental state of their parents but also general material living conditions. Over-indebted families may be evicted or lose their home as a result of foreclosure. This may cause strong psychological pressure for children, even if that remains a threat and not an actual event. The children cannot be sure whether they can keep their familiar neighbourhood, school and hobbies, together with friends and acquaintances attached to them.

Despite the fact that the pathway mechanisms linking parental debt problems with children's well-being are easy to identify and that the problem of reverse causality is not as big as with the parents, there is very little research on intergenerational effects of over-indebtedness. With data from the city of Philadelphia in the US, Crosnoe et al. suggest that economically disadvantaged parents are less optimistic about their adolescents' educational opportunities, which results in later enrolment in higher education. In response to financial constraints, they engage less in the proactive parenting that encourages enrolment. Crosnoe et al. (2002, p. 700) conclude that "this lack of hope can be self-fulfilling, interfering with positive parenting in ways that negatively affect the adolescent's transition to adulthood". Berger and Houle (2016) demonstrated that in the US higher levels of home mortgage and education debt were associated with greater socio-emotional well-being for children, whereas higher levels of and increases in unsecured debt were associated with lower levels of and declines in child socio-emotional well-being.

Mykyta has studied the effects of the housing market crash in the mid-2000s on families and children in the US. The crash was characterized by unusually high rates of mortgage delinquencies and foreclosures. A large number of families faced the prospect of losing their homes. Mykyta (2015) showed that families experiencing foreclosure had lower incomes; experienced greater hardship and food insecurity; had higher odds of accessing the public safety net; and were less likely to receive support from private safety nets than their counterparts. The changes in foreclosure status were associated with reduced economic well-being, increased hardship and food insecurity. In another study Mykyta (2014) used individual foreclosure event data linked to the Survey of Income and Program Participation to examine the effects of foreclosure on child well-being. According to the results, children whose families experienced foreclosure had lower levels of economic well-being and participation in extracurricular activities, more schooling mobility and less frequent praise and time spent with parents. However, changes in foreclosure status were only associated with changes in poverty status and receipt of non-cash assistance from public safety net programmes.

Two studies in Finland analysed the association between parental over-indebtedness and children's depression and receipt of social assistance (a minimum income programme in Finland) with 1987 cohort data. The parents had become over-indebted during the economic crisis in the early 1990s and were over-indebted for more than 15 years (see Blomgren et al. 2016). The first study showed that the children of over-indebted families had elevated risk of depression after controlling for a number of previously known risk factors for depression (Tanskanen

2015). The second study demonstrated that parental over-indebtedness was associated with children's receipt of social assistance, especially long-term use of social assistance (Lehtonen 2016).

EFFECTS OF DEBT-RELATED STIGMA: SOCIETAL CONSEQUENCES

General trust

Earlier research has demonstrated that the level of trust in a society has consequences for economic performance as well as for individual well-being (Fukuyama 1995). Countries which display high degrees of trust in all dimensions (in their national institutions and in their countrymen and women) are also the most competitive (Hiilamo and Kangas 2013). There seems to be a "good circle" between the increasing social trust and various subjective measures of welfare, while there is a vicious circle with decreasing social trust (Fridberg and Kangas 2008).

Over-indebtedness can lead to a number of important negative effects on the whole of society, such as poverty growth, low social cohesion, loss of confidence in the financial industry and reductions in loan offers, even for solvent borrowers. As described above, over-indebtedness is associated with social exclusion and deprivation since it inhibits the consumption that is often a required component in everyday social activities. It is also related to disruption of family ties and social networks. The stigma of over-indebtedness may eventually not only affect the health and well-being of the delinquent borrower. With all these effects combined it also reduces social trust and mutual support in the community.

In the CPEC (2013, p. 173) study the stakeholders considered as the most important consequence of over-indebtedness the loss of consumer confidence in the financial industry. That was most likely due to the fact that representatives of the financial industry were also interviewed as stakeholders. As described above, the financial industry is generally held responsible for the onset of massive consumer over-indebtedness after the Global economic crisis. With eight household surveys from the Netherlands between 2006 and 2013, van Cruijsen et al. (2016) showed that respondents' personal adverse financial crisis experiences did not only reduce their trust in banks, but also had an immediate negative effect on general trust.

Also, more widespread cynicism and frustration with the political system was expressed in the CPEC interviews. The specific comments concerned the negative effects of over-indebtedness on public morale, rising crime, emigration, frustration with the political system and reduced social cohesion. One respondent noted that "people blame the politicians that they are serving the interests of the banks" (CPEC 2013, p. 199). In a similar way, one respondent from Germany noted that the perception of unfairness boils down to the fact that insolvent banks were rescued by the state for billions of euros during the euro crises while "normal citizens" were "left high and dry" by the state.

Analysing Norwegian over-indebted individuals, Poppe related the lack of trust as a result of over-indebtedness to the widespread shame, following the neglect of repayment norm, that his informants felt throughout the process, from first repayment difficulties to a settled life as over-indebted individuals. Since there is no silver bullet for those with serious debt problems to escape debts, the coping is wrapped up in an ambience of disappointment and dismay. Poppe (2008, p. 199) argues that falling short of approval and never obtaining a real breakthrough goes beyond feelings of cynicism towards established institutions. It also triggers sentiments that go well into the realms of anger and distrust. Poppe (2008, pp. 189–192) also observed that some default-debtors attributed their situation to false accusations, conspiracy and fraud allegations. Poppe's informants made references to a business partner's fraud in not paying VAT, false accusations of paedophilia by an ex-wife, and a real estate agent's deception. These default-debtors, together with those who blamed bad luck, had a tendency to express distrust of specific others – creditors, representatives of welfare systems and political bodies. They were also disappointed with the welfare system, which is a cornerstone of the Norwegian institutional setting. In some cases, the mistrust develops into a hostility which may result in desperate action towards the public institutions.

There is some empirical evidence to show that financial crises bring about political instability. Using World Values Survey (WVS) data for 60 countries, Mian et al. (2013) showed that countries become more politically polarized and fractionalized following financial crises. The authors argue that voters become more ideologically extreme and ruling coalitions become weaker, reducing the likelihood of major financial reforms precisely when they might have especially large benefits.

Innovation Potential

A substantial number of over-indebted individuals have accrued their debts from entrepreneurial activity or self-employment (for example Poppe et al. 2016). The experience of failure is discouraging for the concerned individuals, but it may also have societal consequences.

Entrepreneurs have a central role in the capitalist system. The birth of new business operations and the demise of old ones is a natural and necessary process. Many companies would not have achieved success if their owners had given up after a first attempt. The feeling of failure as a result of over-indebtedness is likely to discourage new innovations.

Running a business is, to some extent, always a gamble. An entrepreneur naturally has to reckon with defaulted payments and external change such as political decisions, changes in patterns of consumption and changes in the state of the economy, which can lead to reduction or complete loss of income for the entrepreneur. Social risk affecting employees, for example illness or separation, can hit entrepreneurs especially hard. It is often difficult for an entrepreneur who has suffered a financial loss to bounce back. A failure that results in a serious and capable entrepreneur being unable or unwilling to make a fresh start also means that the society loses new enterprises that could have created economic growth (SOU 2014). An econometric study involving 15 countries by Armour and Cumming (2008) showed that bankruptcy laws that are more entrepreneur friendly give rise to statistically and economically significant increases in self-employment per population.

As a sign of an emerging narrative on fresh starts for over-indebted entrepreneurs, Sweden prepared an official inquiry to present proposals that give entrepreneurs who are personally liable for debts that have arisen in their business activities broader opportunities for debt restructuring (SOU 2014).

Public Expenditures

The CPEC (2013, pp. 197–200) study highlighted several items of public spending which tend to increase as a result of over-indebtedness. They include health care services, costs for providing houses for those who lost their homes through home repossession, free legal aid for insolvent persons and costs for provision of debt advice services. The relationship between debt and unemployment also necessitates more spending on unemployment benefits (Eurofound 2012). It has been calculated that in the UK the average cost per debt problem to the public and in lost economic output is over 1000 pounds, with serious problems costing many times more (Pleasence et al. 2007).

COUNTRY-SPECIFIC CONSEQUENCES

Can we relate the consequences of over-indebtedness to different debt discharge or welfare state regimes? Using EU-SILC data, Angel (2016) studied the effects of different personal insolvency regimes in Europe regarding over-indebtedness on subjective health. Surprisingly, there were hardly any differences in the effect of over-indebtedness on health among debt discharge regimes for the arrears indicator; but for the at risk of over-indebtedness (AROI) indicator the effect on health was strongest in countries where discharge regulations are most debtor-friendly. Angel attributed the results to selection effect where debtor-friendly regimes would incentivize already over-indebted households to borrow more. However, the author called for more research on the topic. In this study, Angel included panel data for three countries discussed in this book, namely Finland, Norway and the UK. In a logit model with Belgium as a reference country, with over-indebtedness measured both through arrears and AROI the respondents in the UK reported better health, while there was no statistically significant effect in Finland or in Norway.

The large European study on over-indebtedness gives qualitative information about which consequences of over-indebtedness the affected persons considered most substantial (CPEC 2013, pp. 8–10). In the UK, the consumers referred most frequently to reduced standard of living. Households reported that they were forced to cut back on all luxuries, such as eating out or going on holiday. Several households also described deteriorated well-being and mental health. More than half of interviewed consumers reported suffering from stress, while around a third mentioned that the stress of their financial situation had placed serious strain on their relationships with their partners. Similarly, the interviewees in Germany most often mentioned reduced standard of living and deteriorating well-being/mental health. In both countries, the informants also made references to financial exclusion.

In the absence of any additional comparative analysis we may only rely on the material presented above and give tentative examples of which consequences could play out more pronouncedly in some countries than in others. Given the limited literature on individual and societal consequences, we discuss both dimensions simultaneously. As countries with high standards of living and poor social protection, we may assume that over-indebtedness limits social participation in the US and UK more than in continental countries (see Table 4.3). We can also speculate that over-indebtedness comes with financial exclusion more often in the US, the UK and Germany, where a bad credit history can prevent people from opening a bank account (CPEC 2013, p. 183). Over-indebtedness is more likely to reduce human capital investments in the US and UK, where institutions of higher education charge high tuition fees. This statement needs to be taken with caution since no actual study was found on the topic.

As to mental and physical health, it seems that there are no major differences across countries with regard to stress caused by over-indebtedness. However, being overweight and smoking were identified as specific consequences of over-indebtedness in Germany (Münster et al. 2009; Rueger et al. 2013). In the Netherlands a study by van Cruijsen et al. (2016) showed that personal financial problems were related to reduced general trust, which indicated that over-indebtedness has a negative impact on general trust. For Finland, the specific consequences identified were the risk of disability retirement (Blomgren et al. 2017), over-indebted parents' children's use of antidepressants (Tanskanen 2015) and receipt of social assistance (Lehtonen 2016). In the review presented above we were not able to identify any study focusing particularly on the consequences of over-indebtedness in Norway (see Poppe 2008, p. 26).

Table 4.3   Country-specific individual and societal consequences of over-indebtedness

Country	Consequence
US	Limited social participation
	Financial exclusion
	Reduced human capital investment
UK	Limited social participation
	Financial exclusion
	Reduced human capital investment
Germany	Financial exclusion
	Over-weight
	Smoking
Netherlands	Reduced general trust
Finland	Disability retirement
	Children's use of antidepressants
	Children's receipt of social assistance

5. How to prevent and alleviate debt problems

To some, over-indebtedness means devastation. To others, it may offer a solution to a problem through bankruptcy, debt settlement or repayment of debt, and a means to move on with life. Rembrandt clearly falls into the latter category (Crenshaw 2006). He was forced to sell his house and most of his possessions, but he met no lasting punishment from either municipal or church authority. He was not compelled to leave town permanently. Due to the financial settlement linked to the will of his deceased wife Saskia, Rembrandt was initially unable to marry his lover Hendrickje Stoffels, but they remained together until Hendrickje's death. The bankruptcy did not discourage Rembrandt from continuing his artistic career. The paintings and prints produced after the bankruptcy include some of the master's most acclaimed works. According to Crenshaw, Hendrickje helped Rembrandt organize his life and prevented his downfall after the bankruptcy.

Modern societies encompass a number of policies and programmes to prevent over-indebtedness and to alleviate its consequences. In many cases the policies have a piecemeal approach which is poorly integrated with all necessary dimensions of the problems. The CPEC (2013, pp. 235–238) study discussed measures to prevent and alleviate over-indebtedness: from providing financial education to income support; enforcing responsible lending; establishing good practices for lenders/creditors; engaging creditors/lenders; providing debt advice; preventing evictions, offering out-of-court procedures for debt settlement and collective debt settlement; legislating procedures for the discharge of debts; and implementing responsible debt collection practices and preventing financial exclusion.

Unfortunately, there is very little systematic research and comparative research in the area. Angel and Heitzmann (2015) tried to analyse the household- and country-level determinants of over-indebtedness by paying attention also to national policies targeted to prevent and alleviate debt problems. After drawing on a multitude of publications as well as secondary and primary data sources they were confronted by a lack of data for a large number of countries, the low quality of the available data or data that was not comparable across countries. For example, the authors did not find any information on irresponsible lending. Given the lack of comprehensive data on the topic, the following discussion will be brief and touch upon a limited number of policies.

The previous chapters analysed the causes and consequences of over-indebtedness. To put it simply: *reversing the causes of over-indebtedness can help prevent it, while policies to tackle the consequences of debt problems may assist in alleviating them.*

In the following, we first discuss prevention of over-indebtedness and then focus on policies to alleviate debt problems (Table 5.1). Given the pervasive nature of debt in modern society it is not likely that debt problems can be prevented in total. However, the difference in the level and volume of debt problems over time and place shows that with effective remedies a large share of debt problems could be thwarted. We focus on three policy areas: namely, regulating financial markets, good lending practices and improving financial literacy. With regard to alleviating the consequences of over-indebtedness, we discuss swift debt discharge, debt counselling, debt collection practices and, finally, welfare state policies. The emphasis is on the swift debt discharge.

Table 5.1   Credit-based social policy framework to prevent and alleviate over-indebtedness

Dimension	Policies
Preventing over-indebtedness	Regulating financial markets Good lending practices Improving financial literacy
Alleviating debt problems	Swift debt discharge Debt counselling Debt collection practices Welfare state policies

PREVENTING OVER-INDEBTEDNESS

Regulating Financial Markets

As demonstrated above, over-indebtedness is strongly associated with economic cycles (e.g. Igan et al. 2012). An overheated economy creates false impressions of uninterrupted growth and leads to household debt levels which prove unsustainable when the tide turns. Stable macroeconomic conditions help prevent over-indebtedness. This is the iron-clad lesson learned after each and every boom to bust cycle. The painful memories, however, tend to fade soon.

As a related problem, there is currently a higher growth rate on return on capital than on wages (Piketty 2014). This is a perpetuating and worsening factor with regard to income and wealth inequalities in society. Consequently, there have been calls to demand a clearer contribution to shared prosperity from the financial sector. In the aftermath of the Global economic crisis, the primary goal and service function of the financial sector in the economy was questioned. There were demands for curbing and reorienting financial flows that dominate financial markets and to end the paradigm of "private profits, social losses" in the banking sector. In the area of financial services, a Financial Transaction Tax (FTT), a Financial Activity Tax (FAT) or ending the absence of VAT on financial services were mentioned as possibilities of taking steps in that direction (Piketty 2014).

The most effective controls against overheating relate to regulation of financial markets where the bubbles are born (Igan et al. 2012). Raising capital and liquidity requirements in banks will help bring stability to the banking sector in the long term, admittedly, however, at a short-term cost of reduced liquidity. Banking regulation is an important solution to prevent consumer over-indebtedness (Dewatripont and Tirole 2012). Banks may not engage in overly aggressive credit marketing if the incentives for banks is adherence to stronger transparency rules and curtailing of excessive accumulation of money and debt through increased capital requirements alongside incentivizing equity-based financing before debt-based financing. Banks serving the routine needs of small customers could be separated from banks engaging in a plethora of other business.

Banking crises accompanied by household over-indebtedness can be attributed to three central characteristics – commonly referred to as bad luck, bad banking and bad policies – which are all completely beyond the influence of individual debtors. The consequences of economic crises on individual debtors are also caused by failures in the governance of the crises (Kjellman 1996). Governance refers to institutional and organizational structures that regulate and coordinate different aspects of socio-economic processes in ways that impact on the allocation, monitoring and enforcement of fiscal and other resources between different stake- and shareholders. The complex power structures between financial sector actors, regulators and politicians have prevented measures which could have alleviated the burden of financial crises on individual debtors. Consumer debtors have been infuriated by the perception of unequal treatment of their obligations and the obligations of big financial institutions.

After the Global economic crises, it has become widely accepted that regulation of the financial sector must be "responsible" in the sense that it includes protection against over-indebtedness of consumers (World Bank 2013b). With regard to credit regulation, there are two competing narratives. The passive credit view claims that there is little that regulation can accomplish. According to this narrative, bubbles should be treated like earthquakes: policy makers should not struggle to regulate markets and stop bubbles, which are not easily identified, but should instead clean up the damage left behind when they burst (Foote et al. 2012). This view is reminiscent of a doctrine often associated with policy adopted by Alan Greenspan, the influential chairman of the Federal Reserve of the United States (the Fed). Meanwhile, the credit supply narrative argues that a consistent pre-bubble pattern can be identified from the data (Mian and Sufi 2015a, pp. 167–187). Debt-fuelled asset price increases, especially in real estate, typically end badly, and should therefore raise a red flag for regulators. The credit supply view suggests that regulation is necessary to make busts less painful. Policies such as macro-prudential regulation and more equity-based loan contracts may help reduce the amplitude of real estate booms.

Mian and Sufi (2015a, pp. 167–187) advocate more flexible student loan and mortgage loan contracts where the creditor would share some of the risk associated with lower return on human capital investment (unemployment) and depreciation of housing assets. In the UK and Australia students already pay a fixed share of their income to pay down student loans. The idea has also been proposed in Finland (Hiilamo 2011). With regard to mortgages, a flexible loan contract would entail reducing the mortgage if house prices fall. In the opposite case, lenders would also benefit from rising house prices (Mian and Sufi 2015a, pp. 169).

Dewatripont and Tirole (2012) emphasize the need for policies to validate managerial choices following good performance in the banking sector, while bad banking practices should be punished. The regulatory policies could include a set of incentives for loan officers, not based on the amount of loans allocated but on the risk of these loans. There is also a need for incentives to determine more precisely the borrower's repayment capacity. They could include strict limits on the maximum debt amount per borrower, as well as clear rules for loan renewals.

Regulating financial market, battling constantly with the ethos of greed and panic, is not easy. Take for example the low interest rate environment dominant for the past Global economic recession period. The relation between interest rate and borrowing capacity is vastly non-linear. In addition, the borrowing capacity increases with the duration of the mortgage, when the interest rates fall. For example, a 50-year mortgage at a rate of 4 per cent allows borrowing almost three times the amount that could be borrowed at a rate of 12 per cent over 20 years (André 2016). A dangerous bubble was created with the lengthening of mortgage maturities during the boom preceding the Global economic crisis. Policies to prevent excess mortgage borrowing should not only focus on loan to value caps but should also take into account changes in maturities.

Good Lending Practices

Good lending practices are also needed to avoid debt problems. In a report for the European Commission (2008a), researchers identified policies that protect consumers from irresponsible lending. They include, among others, the implementation of credit-scoring schemes, credit reports and usury laws. In the CPEC (2013, p. 14) study, the most commonly reported preventive measure was to require lenders to comply with responsible lending provisions in order to assess the creditworthiness of prospective borrowers. A 2014 EU Consumer Credit Directive (2014/17/EU) as well as national regulations set out provisions for assessing the creditworthiness of prospective borrowers. They include criteria for ratios of loan service burden to income. These regulations aim to ensure that arrears are prevented and households are still able to make ends meet. Many countries have credit registers which can be consulted before granting loans.

Good lending practices entail controlling for the type of products that are offered to various borrowers. For example, loans with deferred repayment designed for young professionals with good prospects of rising income were offered also to low-income households before the financial collapse of 2008 (André 2016). Financial institutions have traditionally granted low-documentation loans to self-employed people who could not document a steady stream of income. These types of loans were also used to increase borrowing among salaried workers, with the risk that they would overstate their income.

Consumers need special protection in the mortgage credit market, where over-indebtedness can have devastating consequences for consumers in terms of eviction and the loss of their home, and for the economy as a whole in terms of financial crises. EU Directive 2014/17/EU concerning consumer mortgage credit agreements contained a number of regulatory tools which in most legal systems in the world would be considered duties of "responsible lending". They include information requirements, duties placing responsibility on lenders and prescriptive solutions with regard to loan-to-value (LTV) and loan-to-income (LTI) ratios. However, the Directive leaves much room for differentiation between the Member States in implementing the duties in national regulation. According to Mak (2015), the Directive's provisions aim at minimum harmonization rather than full harmonization.

Credit reporting systems reduce information asymmetries between borrowers and lenders. Creditors are likely to deny credit to individuals with problematic credit histories, thereby also protecting the latter from irresponsible lending. However, the problem with credit registers is that they may contain false information and can be used for inappropriate purposes, for example to disqualify job applicants. The financial industry in Europe is keen on implementing positive credit reporting systems that would help creditors measure how well consumers manage their finances and how much debt they have. In essence, the US already has a positive credit reporting system where long-term customer and good payment history improve chances for better loans. The current system, for example, in Finland is primarily based on negative credit reporting of debt enforcement information (Majamaa et al. 2017).

The UK credit rules implemented after the Global economic crises seek to ensure access to the mortgage market for those who can afford it, while bringing to an end the poor mortgage practices of previous years when almost anyone qualified for a mortgage (Mak 2015). The new rules include stricter duties of responsible lending imposed on lenders and will place more responsibility on the creditors, with possible preventive effects. On the other hand, positive reporting could lead to financial exclusion among those who have, for one reason or another, defaulted at some point in life. The new rules in the UK have left many households with lower or erratic incomes with no source of affordable credit for unexpected needs, and a consequent growth in very high-interest money-lenders with questionable ethics.

The discussion on good lending practices has been focused on bank loans and, more specifically, on mortgages, while the lending practices of other types of creditors have received less attention. Good lending practices should cover not only banks and established financial institutions but also companies offering non-secured loans. Regulation should indeed look beyond general usury laws into financial innovations and product development at the bottom of the credit market. That entails especially payday loans and similar products. In Finland, a legislative reform came into force in 2013 – the Finnish Consumer Protection Act, Chapter 7 – which included an interest rate cap on so-called instant loans

(Oksanen et al. 2015). The reform practically killed the market for small loans, most commonly a couple of hundred euros, which in many cases had annual interest rates to 1000 per cent and above. However, there is evidence that the same creditors moved on to larger high-interest unsecured loans, which are aggressively marketed to the same segment of low-income individuals (Majamaa et al. 2017).

Several US states also have interest caps for payday lending and other types of subprime lending options (Soederberg 2014). Online subprime lending markets are seriously undermining state-level regulation, though. In those states where caps are in place, companies have tried to sidestep regulations by structuring payday loans as instalment loans. Given the particulars of the customers, these products are, in essence, structured to fail. The problem in imposing interest rate caps and similar measures is that these measures do not tackle the root causes of the problem, which are lack of money and absence of other credit alternatives. People using payday loans may have tapped all other sources of credit, including help from family or friends, before turning to payday lenders.

Improving Financial Literacy

Promotion of financial literacy has emerged as an individual-based measure to prevent over-indebtedness. Among the individual causes of over-indebtedness discussed in Chapter 3 it would not only address financial illiteracy but also reckless spending and risky investments. Focus on financial literacy is grounded on the fact that people lack the skills and capabilities to make financial decisions. A wide range of money management topics relate to financial literacy, which is a broad term covering money management skills needed by both the rich and the poor. Apart from investment education they also include, for example: measuring financial fitness; understanding loans and credit; assessing retirement income needs; stretching the dollar; understanding life insurance and health insurance; buying a home within one's means; and financial planning for families with special needs.

As discussed earlier, behavioural economics has demonstrated that short-sightedness and unreasonable risk-taking can lead people into debt problems (Anderloni and Vandone 2011). The inherent problems in people's financial decision-making are a fact (Webley and Nyhus 2001). However, financial literary education may have a political dimension. In contrast to lender liability view, which recognizes the more advantageous position of creditors, financial literacy justifies the shifting of greater financial risk (for example on credit card debt, mortgage, tuition fees, health care costs and so on) to individuals from corporations and governments. Thereby the lack of financial literary can be interpreted as a cause of over-indebtedness. If the problem is actually caused by irresponsible lending, this type of financial literacy discourse may cast the blame on the victim. The discourse bears a resemblance to the old-fashioned notion of debt as an individual problem where individual inadequacy is stressed.

Fortunately, more critical financial literacy education is also available (Kilborn 2005). In this case the literacy education focuses on pitfalls and injustices in the credit markets and allows individuals to better understand the system and avoid problems. Kilborn argues that financial literacy education based on behavioural economic research could be helpful in preventing debt problems. It should raise awareness of one's biases or tendencies to over-borrow and of the many new products designed to mitigate them (commitment contracts, behaviourally informed personal financial management software, etc.). Poppe (2008) contends that financial literacy interventions should be aimed at improving knowledge levels in the weak group of debtors. Earlier studies have established young people and poorly educated people as risk groups. Financial literacy studies have shown that there are gender differences in financial knowledge and behaviour (Lusardi and Mitchell 2014). Women tend to score lower on knowledge but higher on behaviour. Empirical research has also shown a clear association between financial literacy and debt management. However, the causal evidence is still weak (Lusardi and Mitchell 2014). More research is also needed to demonstrate which policies and programmes could cost-effectively increase financial literacy.

Both international organizations and national governments have tried to promote financial literacy. In 2003, the OECD started an intergovernmental project with the specific objective to improve financial education and literacy standards through the development of common financial literacy principles; and in 2008, it launched the International Gateway for Financial Education. Its objective is to serve as a clearinghouse for financial education programmes, information and research worldwide.

The US government established the Financial Literacy and Education Commission under the Financial Literacy and Education Improvement Act in 2003 (Rogers et al. 2015). The Commission published its National Strategy on Financial Literacy in 2006. In 2010, the US Congress passed the Dodd-Frank Wall Street Reform and Consumer Protection Act (Dodd-Frank Act), which created the Consumer Financial Protection Bureau (CFPB). The CFPB has the mandate to promote financial education through its Consumer Engagement and Education group. Also in the US, a collection of national corporate, academic, non-profit and government non-profit organizations are working to improve financial education. A number of (UK) charities – such as MyBnk, The Money Charity (formerly Credit Action), the Talking Economics Project, Citizens Advice Bureau and Young Money (formerly Personal Finance Education Group) – offer education on financial literacy. In the UK, the Financial Services Act 2010 included a provision to establish the Consumer Financial Education Body, which in 2011 was rebranded as the Money Advice Service (Mak 2015).

Development of banking and finance regulations and investments in financial literacy do not, alas, eradicate poverty and poor people's inherent need for credit. People with low incomes still need alternative sources of credit if they cannot operate in the markets. This problem can be addressed by guaranteeing access to credit for the most vulnerable parts of society. There is an urgent need to develop non-commercial credit alternatives for people with limited financial means. A large number of municipalities, NGOs and faith-based actors already issue emergency loans for poor households, but the social credit system is still underdeveloped in relation to questionable semi-official and unofficial lending sectors. In responding to the situation, churches in some parts of Europe have made a concrete and practical decision by supporting a Churches' Mutual Credit Union (Conference of European Churches 2017, p. 114).

ALLEVIATING DEBT PROBLEMS

If and when economies get into crisis, macro-economic policies such as monetary easing and fiscal transfers to overburdened households are crucial elements of forestalling excessive contractions in economic activity, increasing unemployment and over-indebtedness (Igan et al. 2012). As general policies to alleviate debt problems, fiscal transfers to households through social safety nets are needed to boost households' incomes, improve their ability to service debt and further help prevent self-reinforcing cycles of rising defaults, declining house prices and lower aggregate demand. Igan et al. (2012) emphasize in particular the "bold and well-designed" household debt restructuring programmes implemented in the United States in the 1930s and in Iceland in 2008.

The systematic nature of economic crises warrants discussion on how to alleviate their consequences on general trust, which is eroded especially through the fact that the crises lead a significant part of the population into over-indebtedness. Trust in public institutions is important both for general well-being and economic performance (Fukuyama

1995). It enables societies to function better and more effectively to accomplish various tasks. As a result of large-scale household debt crisis people's faith in public institutions such as courts, tax authorities, financial regulators and politicians may collapse (Fridberg and Kangas 2008). In the case of large-scale crises, a viable way to improve the economy and increase general trust would be directly giving money to individuals in the form of a debt jubilee.

A similar argument is given by the Conference of European Churches (CEC 2017), which calls for policies for a fresh start and restoration of productive capacity. The CEC document on European economic governance references the book of Deuteronomy (15:1–23): "At the end of every seven years you shall grant a release. And this is the manner of the release: every creditor shall release what he has lent to his neighbour." CEC (2017, p. 113) admits that it is challenging to strike a balance between the interests or the debtors, creditors and the society:

> Needless to say, in the contemporary economy with a large (and perhaps excessive) financial sector the question of restoration and restriction is not an easy one. Also, we realize that social justice is not always and automatically best served by debt cancellations. After all, creditors also deserve legal protection and responsibility always needs to be seen in conjunction with solidarity. In the end, economic restructurings need to be pursued keeping in mind a real and productive restoration of the debtor's productive capacities, but also the rights of the creditors.

Swift Debt Discharge

Consumer bankruptcy remains the most important means of tackling consumer over-indebtedness and reintegrating debt-ridden households. In economic terms, the availability of debt settlement is a type of "mandatory debt insurance". It transfers the risk of default in consumer credit markets from debtors to their creditors. The rationale is that the creditors are, as opposed to debtors, "superior risk assessors" and "superior risk bearers" (Ramsay 2017, p. 160). Especially the banks and their shareholders are generally more able to bear the risks of default than over-indebted homeowners. The creditors may rely on credit reporting and credit scoring to estimate the likelihood of default and adjust their lending standards accordingly. By raising the price of credit, they can also pool the costs of default and spread these costs among borrowers (Heuer 2013).

Debt discharge is available in all countries covered in this book, and in most developed countries in general. However, there are big differences in repayment obligations and payment periods before discharge is possible (see Table 2.6 for examples). Time frames range from a couple of months in the US to three or five years in continental Europe (or ten years for mortgage debtors who wish to retain their property in Finland). Heuer (2013) argues that a majority of over-indebted households in several European countries are excluded from a financial fresh start. Heuer attributes this to moral, economic and social-political foundations ingrained in consumer bankruptcy legislation which render these systems unfair and inefficient. Ramsay (2017) describes an emerging European model of personal insolvency of three to five years, with discharge of remaining debt at the end of the period.

Personal insolvency regimes can be analysed in combination with welfare state orientations. It seems obvious that the comparatively generous consumer bankruptcy legislation in the US is compensating for the lack of comprehensive welfare state policies. Without the opportunity for a "fresh new" start through Charter 7 or 13 of the Bankruptcy Code the over-indebted individual in the US would be (even more than currently) doomed to permanent poverty. In Europe, the social contract embedded in welfare state policies includes not only more generous social benefits but also, in the case of over-indebtedness, more stringent obligations (Heuer 2013). In effect, these obligations favour the creditors, who in many default cases avoid total loss of capital and interest through payments which the debtors make from their social security benefits, most notably unemployment and pension payments. With little exaggeration, it can be argued that as long as the legislation prevents personal bankruptcy the welfare state is subsidizing the financial sector through entitlements to over-indebted individuals and households.

The most obvious solution to debt problems under any circumstances is to offer an escape through personal bankruptcy or debt settlement. Debt discharge can help strike a balance between the interests of the debtors, the creditors and the general public by offering effective intervention and mediation at a critical moment. However, debt discharge involves profound moral, legal, economic and social-political issues. Kilborn (2005), who criticizes the US regime as too lenient on debtors, argues that European legislators have agonized over how best to chart the line between the Scylla of "de-responsibilizing" debtors with "easy" relief and the Charybdis of demanding too much sacrifice, and thereby making payment plans doomed to fail. The strongest argument against easier access to debt relief is the presumptions of widespread abuse by debtors, followed by high credit prices and low credit availability. While it is true that the credit market in the US misses several rungs in the lending ladder between credit cards and small-money products (Kilborn 2005), there is no evidence of large-scale abuse of consumer bankruptcy.

Mian and Sufi (2015a, p. 12) argue that a financial system which thrives on massive use of household debt concentrates risk squarely on debtors, and thereby "actually works *against* us, not *for* us". There is a strong public argument for debt settlement and debt discharge. In effect, debt discharge puts money into the hands of consumers with a high marginal propensity to consume (Mian and Sufi 2015a, p. 163). There are also other practical reasons for advocating swift debt discharge. Creditors' outstanding accounts are very seldom fully settled, despite the fact that social transfers are used for repayment. Society also has to pay for the rehabilitation of the over-indebted by offering a wide range of social and health care services and transfers. Society is also likely to lose over-indebted individuals' contributions in the labour market and in the business sector. The effects of over-indebtedness are also detrimental to employers, who are burdened with the deterioration of work quality and motivation of over-indebted employees. Also, the administration of wage attachment is time-consuming and entails substantial transaction costs for employers. The over-indebted have in many cases several debtors, and organizing repayment is a challenge. Finally, Mian and Sufi (2015a, p. 165) argue that it is the creditor's responsibility to choose the debtor; and if the debtor fails to pay, the creditor should bear the losses.

After the Global economic crisis, policy makers recognized the role of household debt as a major contributing factor. This notion accelerated transnational narratives and policy scripts about the nature and role of personal insolvency. For example, the EU and the IMF required insolvency reforms under loan conditionality rules, and the World Bank Insolvency and Creditors Right Task Force convened to discuss for the first time the issue of consumer insolvency as a systemic risk. In 2013 the World Bank published the *Report, on the Treatment of the Insolvency of Natural Persons,* which made the case for the introduction of personal insolvency discharge on social and economic grounds (World Bank 2013a). Interestingly, the report emphasized that moral hazard was generally a small problem, and a bigger problem was to access bankruptcy despite the stigma attached to it (Ramsay 2017, pp. 152, 165).

As externalities involved in debt default, the World Bank report mentioned lost productivity, cost to family, communities and health care, wasteful collection costs and discouragement of entrepreneurs. With regard to mortgage payment default it also includes significant "deadweight losses" stemming from the neglect and deterioration of properties that sit vacant for months. These properties may not only reduce selling prices for other properties, as described earlier, but they can also have a negative effect on neighbourhood social cohesion and crime (Immergluck and Smith 2006).

The World Bank report drew on European ideas such as prevention of social exclusion and insolvency as a form of social insurance, but was critical of European policies of mandatory requirements for attempts at voluntary settlement (they were considered not cost effective) and long payment plans imposed on individuals with no payment capacity (Ramsay 2017, pp. 156–157).

Effects of Debt Discharge

There is some empirical evidence which shows that debt settlements indeed help alleviate debt problems. By analysing EU-SILC household data for 27 European countries, Angel and Heitzman (2015) showed that debt discharge regimes matter for the level of over-indebtedness. Over-indebtedness was a more serious problem in countries with less lenient debt discharge systems.

However, several studies have shown that bankrupt consumers continue to have financial difficulties. Porter and Thorne (2006) showed that one year after Chapter 7 bankruptcy one-quarter of US debtors were still struggling to pay routine bills, and a third of them were no better off in financial terms than at the time of the bankruptcy. Also, Han and Li (2011) found that bankrupt households were more likely to experience renewed financial difficulties, accumulate less wealth and use expensive credit sources such as payday loans. Financial difficulties persisted even ten years after filing for bankruptcy. The results could be attributed to selection effects. To tackle that problem Dobbie and Song (2015) used a randomized methodology based on the fact that judges vary in their rates of granting bankruptcy protection. The results gave more confirmation of the positive effects of debt discharge. The individuals on the margins whose bankruptcy might randomly be confirmed or rejected showed that over the first post-filing years bankruptcy protection led to very strong increases in income and decreases in mortality and foreclosure. However, the positive result was mostly attributed to the deterioration of outcomes among dismissed filers, not gains by granted filers.

According to Ramsay (2017, p. 177) a more forgiving bankruptcy law is justifiable on humanitarian grounds, but it is still unclear whether it alone contributes to entrepreneurship and economic growth. A more comprehensive welfare state might also encourage risk taking. There is also need for more research on interaction between debt relief with housing policy and other welfare state policies.

In some cases, provisions to enable amicable arrangements outside the courts between creditors and debtors (e.g. formal procedures to set up payment plans) can be more effective than court-based solutions, which in any event involve bureaucracy and cost. This type of precondition gives the creditors a stronger position and adds to time spent with unsustainable debts. Ramsay (2017, p. 196) concludes that individual insolvency is part of a social safety net: "It may be a second-best solution filling in holes in the welfare system but it performs a useful function." However, the voluntary arrangement should not be made contingent upon using court-based solutions.

Adoption of the US Model?

Why have the continental and North European countries not followed the US example in offering swift debt discharge for consumer debts? The idea of swift debt discharge has strong support among academics. For example, Heuer (2013) and Ramsay (2017) advocate for Europe the adoption of the US-style market model of consumer bankruptcy, which would combine economic efficiency with social inclusion. That model would shift the risk of default to commercial creditors, who are clearly in a better position to evaluate the risk of default and can spread its costs through the debtor's premium on credit. In case of default, debtors would receive a quick fresh start – that is, full discharge of their debts – in exchange for relinquishing their (non-exempt) assets and, possibly, a reasonable payment period. Heuer claims that the model would serve both the market and the households, ensuring quick economic reintegration and social participation.

Given the role of the European Union in regulating financial markets, a change in the paradigm of debtor treatment could start from EU level. The European countries have already made preparations in this respect. However, despite sustained efforts the EU has not been successful so far in the harmonization of commercial insolvency law (Ramsay 2017, p. 153). The EU Consumer Credit Directives of 1978 and 2009 did not address consumer over-indebtedness; nor is there any other European Union law instrument that addresses over-indebtedness or insolvency of consumers (Niemi 2012).

Easing the conditions for consumer bankruptcy is likely to provoke opposition from financial institutions and judicial actors. The traditional bank lending view has been the dominant paradigm to fight against consequences of economic crises (Mian and Sufi 2015a). It emphasizes the importance of recapitalizing the banks and not taking any measures that would endanger the banks' stability. Mian and Sufi (2015a, pp. 127, 131) criticize this view with a simple question: "Do we really think that households and companies desperately want to borrow when the entire economy is collapsing around them?" They argue that the flawed bank lending view has remained powerful due to creditors' immense political power and backward economist thinking. According to Mian and Sufi (2015a, p. 134) the bank lending view "advocates taxpayer gifts to exactly those households that need relief the least".

International organizations and governments may be unwilling to implement debt discharge provisions after the Global economic crisis invoked moral hazard (Ramsay 2017, p. 23). However, it is doubtful if homeowners are sophisticated players who could speculate in the market by taking advantage of naive lenders with the specific knowledge that housing prices are inflated (Mian and Sufi 2015a, p. 14). The idea of swift debt discharge is also encountering moral resistance. There are even stronger ethical values at play in consumer insolvency law than in business bankruptcy law (Niemi 2012, p. 458). Swift debt discharge represents a departure from the entrenched moral and social norms of current bankruptcy systems. Politicians and voters tend to object to paying for the "irresponsibility of others". The prejudiced arguments are difficult to counter due to the fact that insolvency law is often an area of quiet politics with low visibility. It is considered as a technical area of little interest to politicians or the public (Ramsay 2017, pp. 13–14).

Underdeveloped personal insolvency systems can also be attributed to civil actor mobilization. The stigma associated with debt is reflected in the absence of collective action among over-indebted individuals. Struggling mortgage holders and other default-debtors are less well politically organized than banks, which is hampering efforts to implement household debt restructuring. As Desmond (2016, p. 180) notes from his study with evicted tenants in Milwaukee: "No one thought the poor more undeserving than the poor themselves." This indicated that social arrangements were interpreted as just and immutable also by the debtors themselves, with no room for mass resistance and to build up collective capacity to change things. According to Desmond (2016, p. 182) "the lack of faith had less to do with their neighbourhood's actual poverty and crime rates than with the level of concentrated suffering they perceived around them". Tenants had a high tolerance for inequality.

Ramsay (2017, pp. 173–179) argues that a new EU narrative is emerging where promotion entrepreneurship and prevention of social and financial exclusion may pave the way for more liberal debt discharge policies. Apart from supporting unfortunate entrepreneurs, there is a strong case for union-level regulation. Currently more and more over-indebted individuals shop for the most debtor-friendly consumer bankruptcy system. There is also evidence to show that over-indebtedness acts as barrier to the free movement of labour. It also needs to be noted that while the market model of personal insolvency may prevent social exclusion as a result of over-indebtedness, it cannot completely solve the problem. It is only a remedy in the event of over-indebtedness, and does not address the root causes of over-indebtedness (Heuer 2013). Personal insolvency as a safety net also individualizes the debt problem and may prevent more collective solutions to the debt problem (Soederberg 2014).

Debt counselling

The remedies available in consumer debt settlement or discharge procedures may not help the over-indebted if they are unable to use them. The debt counselling services are needed to support debtors in the preparation of debt relief proceedings; absorption of costs for the debt relief procedure from public funds; or a waiver for no income, no assets debtors. The universal adoption of a consumer bankruptcy with swift debt discharge would not solve the problem of over-indebtedness automatically. To be effective the legislative reform should be accompanied by regulation guaranteeing availability of professional and low-cost debt counselling services for over-indebted individuals and families (Heuer 2013).

Over-indebted individuals in many cases find it difficult to struggle with multiple creditors and juridical systems they are normally not familiar with. Debt counselling is needed not only for formal consumer bankruptcy procedures but also for informally brokered arrangements with creditors and formal out-of-court debt settlement procedures. Some government officials and charitable actors may also offer official financial support for households in debt. The over-indebted individuals may need advice in seeking help from these programmes. In the CPEC (2013, p. 200) study the stakeholders emphasized the relatively good value for money and low cost to society arising from debt advice and restructuring.

In Germany, some companies have considered providing debt counselling to their employees (Haas 2006). However, mandatory debt counselling enforced in Germany is not always accepted by debtors, who perceive their predicament as a consequence of external factors. Elliehausen et al. (2007) examined the impact of individualized credit counselling delivered to nearly 8000 consumer clients during 1997 in the US. The study showed that recipients of debt advice services relative to a comparison group of uncounselled borrowers were able to reduce their reliance on credit and to use bank accounts more sensibly. Techniques to control for self-selection into counselling revealed that much of the improvement was attributable to characteristics unique to consumers who sought counselling. However, counselling itself was associated with substantial reductions in debt and appeared to provide the greatest benefit to those borrowers who had the least ability to handle credit prior to counselling. Kim et al. (2003) found that debt counselling indirectly affected financial well-being and health in the US. Counselling reduced the financial stressor events of clients who stayed in the programme for 18 months.

The funding of debt advice services remains a problem, though. In the CPEC (2013) study the stakeholders very seldom mentioned any significant or sustained increase in funding for advice services, despite the fact that the financial crises greatly increased the demand for such services. The over-indebted individuals interviewed for the study reported that they were eagerly seeking advice to solve their debt problems.

Debt Collection Practices

Some of the negative consequences of over-indebtedness are directly related to debt collection practices (Fontinelle 2017). Policies that allow for responsible arrears management and debt recovery by lenders (e.g. instruments that help avoid arrears, handle arrears and collect debts) may alleviate the consequences of over-indebtedness. As described above, debt collection is a booming area of business which is sometimes poorly regulated and monitored. In the US, the Federal Trade Commission (2017) enforces the Fair Debt Collection Practices Act (FDCPA), which prohibits deceptive, unfair and abusive debt collection practices. The Act goes into detail in addressing unacceptable debt collection practices. For example, it bars collectors from using obscene or profane language, threatening violence, calling consumers repeatedly or at unreasonable hours, misrepresenting a consumer's legal rights, disclosing a consumer's personal affairs to third parties, and obtaining information about a consumer through false pretences.

Welfare State Policies

Over-indebtedness is strongly associated with changes in the labour market. Unemployment, precarious jobs and low pay lead to debt problems. In the continental welfare states of Germany and the Netherlands comprehensive public policies promote employment and offer social protection for the unemployed and for those who cannot participate in the labour market. That is the case even more so in the Nordic welfare states of Finland and Norway (Hiilamo and Kangas 2013). Despite a relatively high degree of social protection unemployment also remains a central cause of over-indebtedness in continental Europe and among the Nordic countries (Poppe et al. 2016). Improved access to paid labour would help prevent over-indebtedness especially among poorly educated individuals who have comparatively low work intensity.

The fact that key public services such as health care and education are free means that only very few individuals get into debt problems as a result of falling ill or completing education. Medical debts and student loans are important causes of over-indebtedness in the US, and also to some degree in the UK (Sullivan et al. 2000). Chapter 7 and 13 in the US and personal bankruptcy in the UK offer avenues for fresh starts for those who have large unpaid liabilities; but they may not help those individuals and households with smaller loans and unpaid bills. The procedures also have some important restrictions. For example, there is no debt discharge for student loans in the US (Mian and Sufi 2015a, p. 167). Universal access to affordable health care would certainly reduce over-indebtedness in the US. The same goes for reduction in tuition fees and more accessible student loans. As opposed to the UK and the US, in-work poverty is relative low in Finland, Germany, Norway and the Netherlands. In the UK and US, raising minimum income would help low-paid workers escape debt problems. The same goes for improvements in unemployment benefit systems.

6. Conclusions: towards social policy solutions to debt problems

The increase in household debt has led to an over-indebtedness epidemic among the rich countries. Throughout the 2000s, household debt relative to disposable income rose in most OECD countries. In particular, the Global economic crises of the first decade of the 2000s, preceded by easy access to credit, led to a household over-indebtedness epidemic. We have shown that over-indebtedness is associated with intense individual suffering and social ills. The analysis demonstrated a paradox where financialization and increase in household debt has boosted consumption and increase in the standard of living among the indebted households, while debt obligations have also led many to loss of financial control, payment difficulties and over-indebtedness (Poppe et al. 2016).

Still there is no silver bullet to solve the problem since, as the analysis above has demonstrated, the causes of over-indebtedness are deeply embedded in the social and economic practices of the global capitalist system. The particular contexts and trajectories of household over-indebtedness were studied in two Anglo-Saxon countries (the United States and the United Kingdom), two continental European countries (Germany and the Netherlands) and two Nordic countries (Finland and Norway). We also reviewed the features of each jurisdiction in establishing payment default and in providing possible debt discharge.

The term credit-based social policy has been used to denote the practices in Anglo-Saxon welfare state traditions where market-based solutions, commercial credit being one of them, are offered instead of public provision. The pervasive nature of debt and the causes and consequences of over-indebtedness imply that credit-based social policy is applied, more or less explicitly, in all welfare states. Over-indebtedness should be recognized as a social risk which calls for collective solutions across different levels and programmes of collective action. Credit-based social policy calls for measures to solve over-indebtedness holistically and strategically.

An important finding from the comparison was that the differences in personal insolvency regimes do not follow the traditional welfare state regime demarcation lines. For over-indebted individuals, the US offers the best possibility for a fresh new start. Undoubtedly the swift debt discharge options in the US, even with their deficiencies, compensate for the underdeveloped welfare programmes in other areas. However, weaknesses of, for example, health care systems and support for students are important causes of over-indebtedness in the US.

We examined the causes and consequences of over-indebtedness from a social policy perspective, where over-indebtedness is understood as a social risk – that is, a factor endangering or preventing the full participation of individuals in society. The social policy approach calls for a method which would integrate different policy areas relating to over-indebtedness. That entails coordination between different ministries and government agencies dealing with a wide range of topics, from regulation of financial markets to consumer education.

The problem of over-indebtedness is closely linked to wealth inequality. A poor man's debt is a rich man's asset. It is ultimately the rich who are lending to the poor through the financial system (Mian and Sufi 2015a, p. 20). Loans serve an important societal function in promoting human capital investments and owner-occupied housing. Accumulated capital also helps individuals and households face social risks. However, in a heavily mortgaged economy the decline in housing prices hit especially hard those who have the least, and it widens the gap between the rich and the poor (Mian and Sufi 2015a, p. 23). Tax allowances for loans as well as public loan programmes and repayment subsidies should be analysed critically since they may increase uncontrollable and unsustainable indebtedness. It also needs to be taken into account that wealth inequality comes with a destructive feedback loop where the rich invest more money in financial markets. To balance supply and demand for credit the creditor must find new borrowers. As the rich save and the poor borrow, the debt will increase (Miand and Sufi 2015a, p. 193).

No doubt swift debt discharge is the most effective solution to debt problems. An important argument for swift debt discharge is also the fact that creditors are much better insulated against the risk of default than debtors. The rich own the stocks and bonds of the banks. Thereby they also own the loans the bank has made, and the interest payments flow through the financial system to the rich (Mian and Sufi 2015a, p. 21).

The recuperation after the Global economic crises has witnessed again increase in household indebtedness in Europe and in the US (OECD 2017a). The causes lie both in pre-crises trends and in reaction to the crises. Introduction of the euro led to a sudden and large fall in interest rates and the risk of currency depreciation. Financial liberalization and development of the single market in financial services enabled greater cross-border capital flows and financial sophistication (CPEC 2013). The

European Central Bank reacted to the crises by lowering interest rates dramatically. The recovery was slow, partly due to the Greek public debt crises, and interest rates were further cut, in some cases even below zero. With negative real-term interest rates household borrowing, especially through mortgages, became lucrative, driving indebtedness towards new record levels. There is an urgent need to develop social policy solutions to over-indebtedness before the next crisis hits the global market.

References

Adelino, M., Schoar, A. and Severino, F. (2016) 'Loan originations and defaults in the mortgage crisis: The role of the middle class', The Review of Financial Studies, 29 (7), pp. 1635–1670.

Alley, D. E., Lloyd, J., Pagán, J. A., Pollack, C. E., Shardell, M. and Cannuscio, C. (2011) 'Mortgage delinquency and changes in access to health resources and depressive symptoms in a nationally representative cohort of Americans older than 50 years', *American Journal of Public Health*, **101** (12), pp. 2293–2298.

Anderloni, L. and Vandone, D. (2011) 'Risk of over-indebtedness and behavioural factors', in Lucarelli, C. and Brighetti, G. (eds) *Risk Tolerance in Financial Decision Making*. Basingstoke: Palgrave Macmillan, pp. 113–132.

Ando, A. and Modigliani, F. (1963) 'The "life-cycle" hypothesis of savings: Aggregate implications and tests', *American Economic Review*, **53** (1), pp. 55–84.

André, C. (2016) 'Household Debt in OECD Countries: Stylised Facts and Policy Issues', *The Narodowy Bank Polski Workshop: Recent Trends in the Real Estate Market and Its Analysis*. Available at: https://ssrn.com/abstract=2841634.

Angel, S. (2016) 'The effect of over-indebtedness on health: Comparative analyses for Europe', *Kyklos*, **69** (2), pp. 208–227.

Angel, S. and Heitzmann, K. (2015) 'Over-indebtedness in Europe: The relevance of country-level variables for the over-indebtedness of private households', *Journal of European Social Policy*, **25** (3), pp. 331–351.

Arghyrou, M. G., Gregoriou, A. and Kontonikas, A. (2009) 'Do real interest rates converge? Evidence from the European Union', *Journal of International Financial Markets, Institutions and Money*, **19** (3), pp. 447–460.

Armour, J. and Cumming, D. (2008) 'Bankruptcy law and entrepreneurship', *American Law and Economics Review*, **10** (2), pp. 303–350.

Atkinson, T., Cantillon, B., Marlier, E. and Nolan, B. (2002) *Social Indicators: The EU and Social Inclusion*. Oxford: Oxford University Press.

Averett, S. and Smith, J. (2014) 'Financial hardship and obesity', *Economics and Human Biology*, **15**, pp. 201–212.

Baele, L., Farooq, M. and Ongena, S. (2014) 'Of religion and redemption: Evidence from default on Islamic loans', *Journal of Banking & Finance,* **44**, pp. 141–159.

Barron, J. M., Staten, M. and Wilshusen S. (2002) 'The impact of casino gambling on personal bankruptcy filing rates', *Contemporary Economic Policy,* **20** (4), pp. 440–455.

Berger, L. M. and Houle, J. N. (2016) 'Parental debt and children's socio-emotional well-being', *Pediatrics,* **137** (2). doi: 10.1542/peds. 2015-3059.

Betti, G., Dourmashkin, N., Rossi, M. and Yin, Y. (2007) 'Consumer over-indebtedness in the EU: Measurement and characteristics', *Journal of Economic Studies,* **34** (2), pp. 136–156.

Betti, G., Dourmashkin, N., Rossi, M., Verma, V. and Yin, Y. (2001) 'Study of the problem of consumer indebtedness: Statistical aspects'. Final report, European Commission.

Blaszczynski, A. and Farrell, E. (1998) 'A case series of 44 completed gambling-related suicides', *Journal of Gambling Studies,* **14** (2), pp. 93–109.

Blomgren, J. K., Maunula, N. and Hiilamo, H. (2016) 'Over-indebtedness and chronic disease: A linked register-based study of Finnish men and women in 1995–2010', *International Journal of Public Health,* **61** (5), pp. 535–44. doi: 10.1007/s00038-015-0778-4.

Blomgren, J. K., Maunula, N. and Hiilamo, H. (2017) 'Do debts lead to disability pension? Evidence from a 15-year follow-up of 54 000 Finnish men and women', *Journal of European Social Policy,* **27** (2), pp. 109–122.

Bridges, S. and Disney, R. (2010) 'Debt and depression', *Journal of Health Economics,* **29** (3), pp. 388–403.

Britt, S., Grable, J. E., Nelson Goff, B. S. and White, M. (2008) 'The influence of perceived spending behaviors on relationship satisfaction', *Journal of Financial Counseling and Planning,* **19** (1), pp. 31–43.

Brzoska, P. and Razum, O. (2008) 'Indebtedness and mortality: analysis at county and city levels in Germany', *Gesundheitswesen,* **70** (7), pp. 387–392.

Bull, J. (2007) *Cohabitation: The Financial Consequences of Relationship Breakdown.* Norwich: HMSO. Available at: www.gov.uk/government/uploads/system/uploads/attachment_data/file/228881/7182.pdf (Accessed: 28 March 2015).

Bunn, P. and Rostom, M. (2015) 'Household debt and spending in theUK'. Bank of England Working Paper No. 554.

Caju, P., Rycx, F. and Tojerow, I. (2016) *Unemployment Risk and Over-Indebtedness: A Micro-Econometric Perspective.* Discussion Paper No. 9572. Frankfurt: European Central Bank.

Campbell, J., Giglio, S. and Pathak, P. (2011) 'Forced sales and house prices', *American Economic Review*, **101** (5), pp. 2108–2131.

Caplovitz, D. (1963) *The Poor Pay More*. New York: Free Press.

Caplovitz, D. (1974) *Consumers in Trouble: A Study of Debtors in Default*. New York: Free Press.

Caplovitz, D. (1979) *Making Ends Meet: How Families Cope with Inflation and Recession*. Beverley Hills: Sage.

Chang, Y. and Lee, K. Y. (2006) 'Household debt and marital instability: Evidence from the Korean labor and income panel study', *Journal of Family and Economic Issues*, **27** (4), pp. 675–691.

Chapman, H. P. (2006) 'A review of "Rembrandt's Bankruptcy: The Artist, His Patrons, and the Art Market in Seventeenth-Century Netherlands" by Paul Crenshaw'. Available at: http://hdl.handle.net/1969.1/95268.

Claessens, S., Kose, A. and Terrones, M., (2011) 'Financial cycles: What? How? When?' IMF Working Papers, No. 11/76.

Conference of European Churches (2017) *Beyond Prosperity: Churches Bring Dialogue on European Economic Governance to the EU*. Brussels: Conference of European Churches.

CPEC (2013) *The Overindebtedness of European Households: Updated Mapping of the Situation, Nature and Causes, Effects and Initiatives for Alleviating Its Impact*. Final Report, Part 1. Berlin: Civic Consulting of the Consumer Policy Evaluation Consortium. Available at: http://ec.europa.eu/consumers/financial_services/reference_studies_documents/docs/part_1_synthesis_of_findings_en.pdf (Accessed: 28 March 2015).

Crenshaw, P. (2006) *Rembrandt's Bankruptcy: The Artist, His Patrons, and the Art Market in Seventeenth-Century Netherlands*. Cambridge: Cambridge University Press.

Crosnoe, R., Mistry, R. S. and Elder, G. H. Jr. (2002) 'Economic disadvantage, family dynamics, and adolescent enrollment in higher education', *Journal of Marriage and Family*, **64** (3), pp. 690–702.

Crouch, C. (2009) 'Privatised Keynesianism: An unacknowledged policy regime', *British Journal of Politics & International Relations*, **11**, pp. 382–399.

Cuesta, M. B. and Budría, S. (2015) 'The effects of over-indebtedness on individual health'. IZA Discussion Paper No. 8912.

D'Alessio, G. and Iezzi, S. (2013) 'Household over-indebtedness: Definition and measurement with Italian data'. Bank of Italy Occasional Paper No. 149. Available at: http://dx.doi.org/10.2139/ssrn.2243578.

Desmond, M. (2016) *Evicted: Poverty and Profit in the American City*. New York: Broadway.

Dew, J. (2007) 'Two sides of the same coin? The differing roles of assets and consumer debt in marriage', *Journal of Family and Economic Issues,* **28** (1), pp. 89–104.

Dew, J. (2008) 'Debt change and marital satisfaction change in recently married couples', *Family Relations,* **57** (1), pp. 60–71.

Dew, J. (2011) 'The association between consumer debt and the likelihood of divorce', *Journal of Family and Economic Issues,* **32** (4), pp. 554–565.

Dewatripont, M. and Tirole, J. (2012) 'Macroeconomic shocks and banking regulation', *Journal of Money, Credit and Banking,* **44** (s2), pp. 237–254.

Dobbie, W. and Song, J. (2015) 'Debt relief and debtor outcomes: Measuring the effect of consumer bankruptcy protection', *American Economic Review,* **105** (3), pp. 1272–1311.

Dominy, N. and Kempson, E. (2003) *Can't Pay or Won't Pay? A Review of Creditor and Debtor Approaches to the Non-Payment of Bills.* London: Lord Chancellor's Dept.

Drentea, P. and Lavrakas, P. J. (2000) 'Over the limit: The association among health, race and debt', *Social Science and Medicine,* **50** (4), pp. 517–529.

Drentea, P. and Reynolds, J. R. (2012) 'Neither a borrower nor a lender be: The relative importance of debt and SES for mental health among older adults', *Journal of Aging and Health,* **24** (4), pp. 673–695.

Edwards, S. (2003) *In Too Deep: CAB Clients' Experience of Debt.* London: Citizens Advice.

Efrat, R. (2006) 'The evolution of bankruptcy stigma', *Theoretical Inquiries in Law,* **7** (2), pp. 365–392.

Elliehausen, E. G., Lundquist, E. C. and Staten, M. E. (2007) 'The impact of credit counselling on subsequent borrower behaviour', *Journal of Consumer Affairs,* **11** (1), pp. 1–28.

Esping-Andersen, G. (1990) *The Three Worlds of Welfare Capitalism.* Cambridge: Polity.

Euler Hermes (2017) *Collection Practices by Country.* Database of debt collection systems in 44 countries. Available at: www.eulerhermes.com/products-solutions/debt-collection/Land-of-payment/Pages/collections-practices-per-country.aspx.

Eurofound (2012) *Household Debt Advisory Services in the European Union.* European Foundation for the Improvement of Living and Working Conditions. Available at: http://eurofound.europa.eu/sites/default/files/ef_publication/field_ef_document/ef1189en.pdf (Accessed: 28 March 2015).

European Commission (2008a) *Towards a Common Operational European Definition of Overindebtedness.* Brussels: European Commission.

European Commission (2008b) *Financial Services Provision and Prevention of Financial Exclusion*. Brussels: European Commission.

European Consumer Debt Network (2013) 'Tackling household over-indebtedness: Materials from the 6th European conference in Athens', *Money matters,* 10, Available at: http://ecdn.eu/wp-content/uploads/2016/05/MM-10-Y13.pdf.

Fedaseyeu, V. and Hunt, R. M. (2014) 'The economics of debt collection: Enforcement of consumer credit contracts'. FRB of Philadelphia Working Paper No. 15-43.

FDIC (2016) *FDIC National Survey of Unbanked and Underbanked Households*. Washington, DC: Federal Deposit Insurance Corporation.

Federal Trade Commission (2017) 'Debt collection'. Available at: www.ftc.gov/news-events/media-resources/consumer-finance/debt-collection (Accessed: 25 October 2017).

Financial Services Authority (2012) *Mortgage Market Review PS12/16*. London: FSA.

Findikaattori (2017) 'Debtors in enforcement'. Statistics Finland. Available at www.findikaattori.fi/en/35.

Fisher, J. D. and Lyons, A. C. (2006) 'Till debt do us part: A model of divorce and personal bankruptcy', *Review of Economics of the Household,* **4** (1), pp. 35–52.

Fligstein, N. and Goldstein, A. (2012) 'A long strange trip: The state and mortgage securitization, 1968–2010', in Knorr Cetina, K. and Preda, A. (eds) *The Oxford Handbook of the Sociology of Finance*. Oxford: Oxford University Press, pp. 339–356.

Fondeville, N., Özdemir, E. and Ward, T. (2010) 'Over-indebtedness: New evidence from the EU-SILC special module', European Commission, Social Europe Research Note 4.

Fontinelle, A. (2017) 'How the debt collection agency business works'. Available at: www.investopedia.com/articles/personal-finance/121514/how-debt-collection-agency-business-works.asp (Accessed: 3 September 2017).

Foote, C., Gerardi, K. and Willen, P. (2012) *Why Did So Many People Make So Many Ex Post Bad Decisions? The Causes of the Foreclosure Crisis*. Cambridge, MA: National Bureau of Economic Research (NBER).

Ford, J. (2008) *The Indebted Society: Credit and Default in the 1980s*. London: Routledge.

Fridberg, T. and Kangas, O. (2008) 'Social capital', in Ervasti, H., Fridberg, T., Hjerm, M. and Ringdal, K. (eds), *Nordic Social Attitudes in a European Perspective*. Cheltenham, UK and Northampton, MA, USA: Edward Elgar Publishing, pp. 65–85.

Fukuyama, F. (1995) *Trust: The Social Virtues and the Creation of Prosperity*. London: Penguin.

Garcia, J. and Draut, T. (2009) *The Plastic Safety Net: How Households Are Coping in a Fragile Economy*. New York: Demos.

Gathergood, J. (2012a) 'Self-control, financial literacy and consumer over-indebtedness', *Journal of Economic Psychology*, **33** (3), pp. 590–602.

Gathergood, J. (2012b) 'Debt and depression: Causal links and social norm effects', *Economic Journal*, **122** (563), pp. 1094–114.

Georgarakos, D., Lojschova, A. and Ward-Warmedinger, M. E. (2010) *Mortgage Indebtedness and Household Financial Distress*. Frankfurt: European Central Bank.

Gerardi, K., Herkenhoff, K., Ohanian, L. and Willen, P. (2015) 'Can't Pay or Won't Pay? Unemployment, Negative Equity and Strategic Default', *The Review of Financial Studies*, **31** (3), pp. 1098–1131.

Giesselmann, M. (2015) 'Differences in the patterns of in-work poverty in Germany and the UK', *European Societies*, **17** (1), pp. 27–46.

Goode, J. (2009) 'For love or money? Couples' negotiations of credit and debt in low-income families in the UK', *Benefits*, **17** (3), pp. 213–224.

Goode, J. (2012a) 'Brothers are doing it for themselves? Men's experiences of getting into and getting out of debt', *Journal of Socio-Economics*, **41** (3), pp. 327–335.

Goode, J. (2012b) 'Feeding the family when the wolf's at the door: The impact of overindebtedness on contemporary foodways in low-income families in the UK', *Food and Foodways*, **20** (1), pp. 8–30.

Grand, J. L. (2008) 'The giants of excess: A challenge to the nation's health', *Journal of the Royal Statistical Society: Series A (Statistics in Society)*, **171** (4), pp. 843–856.

Gross, D. and Souleles, N. (2001) 'An empirical analysis of personal bankruptcy and delinquency', NBER Working Paper No. 8409.

Grundy, E. and Holt, G. (2001) 'The socioeconomic status of older adults: How should we measure it in studies of health inequalities?' *Journal of Epidemiology and Community Health*, **55** (12), pp. 895–904.

Gulbrandsen, L. (2005) '*Kort vei – til lykke eller ruin? Kredittvekst, betalingsvilje og betalingsevne*', Rapport 14/05. Oslo: Norsk institutt for forskning om oppvekst, velferd og aldring (NOVA).

Gutiérrez-Nieto, B., Serrano-Cinca, C. and de la Cuesta González, M. (2017) 'A multivariate study of over-indebtedness' causes and consequences', *International Journal of Consumer Studies'*, **41** (2), pp. 188–198.

Haas, O. (2006) 'Overindebtedness in Germany', ILO Social Finance Working Paper No. 44.

Hager, E. (2015). *Debtors' Prisons, Then and Now: FAQ*. The Marshall Project. Available at: www.themarshallproject.org/2015/02/24/debtors-prisons-then-and-now-faq (Accessed: 17 November 2017).

Han, S. and Li, G. (2011) 'Household borrowing after personal bankruptcy', *Journal of Money Credit and Banking*, **43** (2–3), pp. 491–517.

Harvey, D. (1978) 'Labour, capital and class struggle around built environment in advanced capitalist societies', in Cox, K. (ed.) *Urbanization and Conflict in Market Societies*. Chicago: Maaroufa Press.

Havlik, R. J., Vukasin, A. P. and Ariyan, S. (1992) 'The impact of stress on the clinical presentation of melanoma', *Plastic and Reconstructive Surgery*, **90** (1), pp. 57–61.

Hay, C. (2011) 'Pathology without crisis? The strange demise of the Anglo-liberal growth model', *Government and Opposition*, **46** (1), pp. 1–31.

Hay, C. (2013) *The Failure of Anglo-Liberal Capitalism*. Basingstoke: Palgrave Macmillan.

Hendrick, S. (1988) 'A generic measure of relationship satisfaction', *Journal of Marriage and the Family*, **50** (1), pp. 93–98.

Henretta, J. C. and Campbell, R. T. (1978) 'Net worth as an aspect of status', *American Journal of Sociology*, **83** (5), pp. 1204–1223.

Heuer, J.-O. (2013) 'Social inclusion and exclusion in European consumer bankruptcy systems'. Paper for the International conference Shifting to Post-Crisis Welfare States in Europe? Long Term and Short Term Perspectives, Berlin, 4–5 June 2013, organized by NordForsk and the Nordic Centres of Excellence NordWel and REASSESS.

Hiilamo, H. (2011) *Uusi hyvinvointivaltio*. Helsinki: Into.

Hiilamo, H., Kangas, O., Fritzell, J., Kvist, J. and Palme, J. (2013), *A Recipe for a Better Life: Experiences from the Nordic Countries*, Helsinki: CMI.

Houle, J. N., Collins, M. J. and Schmeiser, M. D. (2015) 'Flu and finances: Influenza outbreaks and loan defaults in US cities, 2004–2012', *American Journal of Public Health*, **105** (9), pp. e75–e80.

Huls, N., Ackermann, H., Bourgoignie, T., Domont-Naert, F., Haane, B., Van Huffel, M., Reich, N., Reifner, U. and Roseval, L. (1994) *Overindebtedness of Consumers in the EC Member States: Facts and Search for Solutions*. Louvain-la-Neuve: Centre de Droit de la Consommation.

Igan, D., Leigh, D., Simon, J. and Topalova, P. (2012) 'Dealing with household debt', in *World Economic Outlook*, April. Washington, DC: International Monetary Fund, Chapter 3.

Immergluck, D. and Smith, G. (2006) 'The eternal costs of foreclosure: the impact of single-family mortgage foreclosures on property values', *Housing Policy Debate*, **17** (1), pp. 57–79.

International Monetary Fund (2012) *World Economic Outlook*. Chapter 2. Washington, DC: International Monetary Fund.

Isaksen, J., Kramp, P., Sørenson, L. and Sørensen, S. (2011) 'Household balance sheets and debt: An international country study'. Monetary Review, Denmarks Nationalbank.

Jameton, A. (1984) *Nursing Practice: The Ethical Issues*. Upper Saddle River, NJ: Prentice Hall.

Jansen, D.-J., Mosch, R. and van der Cruijsen, C. (2015) 'When does the general public lose trust in banks?', *Journal of Financial Services Research*, **48** (2), pp. 127–141.

Kalela, J., Kiander, J., Kivikuru, U., Loikkanen, H. and Simpura, J. (eds) (2001) *Down from the Heavens, Up from the Ashes: The Finnish Economic Crisis of the 1990s in the Light of Economic and Social Research*. Helsinki: Government Institute for Economic Research.

Karanikolos, M. Mladovsky, P., Cylus, J., Thomson, S., Basu, S., Stuckler, D., Mackenbach, J. and McKee, M. (2013) 'Financial crisis, austerity, and health in Europe', *Lancet,* **381** (9874), pp. 1323–1331. doi: 10.1016/S0140-6736(13)60102-6.

Keese, M. (2009) 'Triggers and determinants of severe household indebtedness in Germany', SOEP Paper No. 239. doi: 10.2139/ssrn.1518373.

Keese, M. (2012) 'Who feels constrained by high debt burdens? Subjective vs. objective measures of household debt', *Journal of Economic Psychology,* **33** (1), pp. 125–141. doi: 10.1016/j.joep.2011.08.002.

Keese, M. and Schmitz, H. (2014) 'Broke, ill, and obese: Is there an effect of household debt on health?', *Review of Income and Wealth,* **60** (3), pp. 525–541.

Kempson, E. (2008) *Over-Indebtedness in Britain*. A report to the Department of Trade and Industry. Personal Finance Research Centre.

Kempson, E., McKay, S. and Willitts, M. (2004) *Characteristics of Families in Debt and the Nature of Indebtedness*. Research Report No 211. Norwich: Department of Work and Pensions.

Kersbergen, K. (1995) *Social Capitalism: A Study of Christian Democracy and the Welfare State*. London: Routledge.

Kiander, J. and Vartia, O. (2011) 'Lessons from the crisis in Finland and Sweden in the 1990s', *Empirica,* **38** (1), pp. 53–69.

Kidger, J., Gunnell, D., Jarvik, J. G., Overstreet, K. A. and Hollingworth, W. (2011) 'The association between bankruptcy and hospital-presenting attempted suicide: A record linkage study', *Suicide Life-Threatening Behavior,* **41** (6), pp. 676–684.

Kiesel, K. and Noth, F (2016) 'When debt spells sin: Does religiosity guard against over-indebtedness?' Paper for Annual Conference (Augsburg): Demographic Change from Verein für Socialpolitik/German

Economic Association. Available at https://EconPapers.repec.org/Re
PEc:zbw:vfsc16:145774.

Kilborn, J. J. (2005) 'Behavioral economics, overindebtedness and comparative consumer bankruptcy: Searching for causes and evaluating
solutions', *Bankruptcy Developments Journal,* **22**, pp. 13–47. doi:
10.2139/ssrn.690826.

Kim, Y., Cancian, M. and Meyer, D. (2015) 'Patterns of child support
debt accumulation', *Children and Youth Services Review,* **51**, pp. 87–
91.

Kim J., Garman, E.T. and Sorhaindo, B. (2003) 'Relationships among
credit counseling clients' financial well-being, financial behaviors,
financial stressor events, and health', *Journal of Financial Counseling
and Planning,* **14** (2), pp. 75–87.

Kjellman A. (1996) *What Can We Learn from the Finnish Banking
Crisis? The Case of the Failures in the Savings Bank Sector.* Turku:
Meddelanden från Ekonomisk-Statsvetenskapliga Fakulteten vid Åbo
Akademi A.

Klein, M. (2016) 'Why is the Netherlands doing so badly?', *Financial
Times,* 16 June.

Korpi, W. and Palme, J. (1998) 'The paradox of redistribution and
strategies of equality: Welfare state institutions, inequality, and poverty
in the Western countries', *American Sociological Review,* **63** (5),
pp. 661–687.

Lazzarato, M. (2012) *The Making of the Indebted Man: An Essay on the
New-Liberal Conditions.* Cambridge, MA: MIT Press.

Lehtonen, I. (2016) *Periytyvätkö velan vaikutukset? Vanhempien ylivel-
kaantumisen yhteys lasten toimeentulotuen saamiseen.* Department
of Social Research. University of Helsinki. Available at: https://
helda.helsinki.fi/handle/10138/167194 (Accessed: 17 June 2018).

Lenton, P. and Mosley, P. (2008) 'Debt and health', Sheffield Economic
Research Paper Series, University of Sheffield.

Logemann, J. (2012) 'From cradle to bankruptcy? Credit access and the
American welfare state', in Logemann, J. (ed.) *The Development of
Consumer Credit in Global Perspective: Business, Regulation, and
Culture.* New York: Palgrave Macmillan, pp. 201–219.

Lusardi, A. and Mitchell, O. (2014) 'The economic importance of
financial literacy: Theory and evidence', *Journal of Economic Literature,* **52** (1), pp. 5–44.

Lynch, J. and Kaplan, G. (2000) *Socioeconomic Position: Social Epidemiology.* New York: Oxford University Press.

Majamaa, K., Sarasoja, L. and Rantala, K. (2017) 'Viime vuosien
muutokset vakavissa velkaongelmissa: Analyysi velkomustuomioista',
Yhteiskuntapolitiikka, 62 (6), pp. 676–686.

Mak, V. (2015) 'What is responsible lending? The EU consumer mortgage credit directive in the UK and the Netherlands', *Journal of Consumer Policy,* **38** (4), pp. 411–430.

Mason, J. W. and Jayadev, A. (2014) '"Fisher Dynamics" in US household debt, 1929–2011', *American Economic Journal: Macroeconomics,* **6** (3), pp. 214–234.

McLaughlin, K. A., Nandi, A., Keyes, K. M., Uddin, M., Aiello, A. E., Galea, S. and Koenen, K. C. (2012) 'Home foreclosure and risk of psychiatric morbidity during the recent financial crisis', *Psychological Medicine,* **42** (7), pp. 1441–1448.

Meltzer, H., Bebbington, P., Brugha, T., Farrell, M. and Jenkins, R. (2013) 'The relationship between personal debt and specific common mental disorders', *European Journal of Public Health,* **23** (1), pp. 108–113.

Melzer, B. (2017) 'Mortgage debt overhang: Reduced investment by homeowners at risk of default', *The Journal of Finance,* **72** (2), pp. 575–612.

Mertens, D. (2017) 'Borrowing for social security? Credit, asset-based welfare and the decline of the German savings regime', *Journal of European Social Policy,* 27 (5), pp. 474–490. doi: 10.1177/0958928717717658.

McEwen, B. S. (1998) 'Protective and damaging effects of stress mediators', *New England Journal of Medicine,* **338**, pp. 171–179.

McEwen, B. S. (2004) 'Protection and damage from acute and chronic stress: Allostasis and allostatic overload and relevance to the pathophysiology of psychiatric disorders', *Annals of the New York Academy of Sciences,* **1032**, pp. 1–7.

McLoyd, V. C. (1990) 'The impact of economic hardship on black families and children: Psychological distress, parenting, and socioemotional development', *Child Development,* **61** (2), pp. 311–346.

Mian, A. and Sufi, A. (2011) 'Consumers and the economy, Part II: Household debt and the weak U.S. recovery', *FRBSF Economic Letter,* 18 January.

Mian, A. and Sufi, A. (2015a) *House of Debt: How They (and You) Caused the Great Recession, and How We Can Prevent It from Happening Again.* Chicago: University of Chicago Press.

Mian, A. and Sufi, A. (2015b) 'Household debt and defaults from 2000 to 2010: Facts from Credit Bureau data'. NBER Working Paper No. 21203. doi: 10.2139/ssrn.2606683.

Mian, A., Sufi, A. and Trebbi, F. (2013) 'Resolving debt overhang: Political constraints in the aftermath of financial crises', *American Economic Journal: Macroeconomics,* **6** (2), pp. 1–28. doi: 10.1257/mac.6.2.1.

Montgomerie, J. (2013) 'America's debt safety-net', *Public Administration*, **91** (4), pp. 871–888.

Mullainathan, S. and Shafir, E. (2013) *Scarcity: Why Having Too Little Means So Much.* New York: Time Books.

Münster, E., Rüger, H., Ochsmann, E., Letzel, S. and Toschke, A. M. (2009) 'Over-indebtedness as a marker of socioeconomic status and its association with obesity: a cross-sectional study', *BMC Public Health*, **9** (286), pp. 1–6.

Murray, C. (1984) *Losing Ground: American Social Policy 1950–1980.* New York: Basic Books.

Muttilainen, V. (2002) *Luottoyhteiskunta: Kotitalouksien velkaongelmat ja niiden hallinnan muodonmuutos luottojen säännöstelystä velkojen järjestelyyn 1980- ja 1990-luvun Suomessa.* Oikeuspoliittisen tutkimuslaitoksen julkaisuja 189. Helsinki: Oikeuspoliittinen tutkimuslaitos.

Mykyta, L. (2014) 'Housing crisis and child well-being: the effects of foreclosure on children and youth'. Presented at the Annual Meetings of the American Sociological Association, San Francisco, CA.

Mykyta, L. (2015) 'Housing crisis and family well-being: Examining the effects of foreclosure on families'. Working Paper No. SEHSD-WP2015-07, US Census Bureau.

Nelson, M. C., Lust, K., Story, M. and Ehlinger, E. (2008) 'Credit card debt, stress and key health risk behaviors among college students', *American Journal of Health Promotion*, **22** (6), pp. 400–407.

Neppl, T. K., Senia, J. M. and Donnellan, M. B. (2016) 'Effects of economic hardship: Testing the family stress model over time', *Journal of Family Psychology*, **30** (1), pp. 12–21.

Niemi, J. (2012) 'Consumer insolvency in the European legal context', *Journal of Consumer Policy*, **35** (4), pp. 443–459.

Niemi-Kiesiläinen, J. (1999) 'Consumer bankruptcy in comparison: Do we cure a market failure or a social problem?' *Osgoode Hall Law Journal*, **37** (1–2), pp. 473–503.

Niemi-Kiesiläinen, J. (2003) 'Collective or individual? Constructions of debtors and creditors in consumer bankruptcy', in Niemi-Kiesiläinen, J., Ramsay, I. and Whitford, W. C. (eds) *Consumer Bankruptcy in Global Perspective.* Oxford: Hart, pp. 41–60.

Niemi-Kiesiläinen, J., Ramsay, I. and Whitford, W. C. (eds) (2003) *Consumer Bankruptcy in Global Perspective.* Oxford: Hart.

Ochsmann, E., Rueger, H., Letzel, S., Drexler, H. and Münster, E. (2009) 'Over-indebtedness and its association with the prevalence of back pain', *BMC Public Health*, **9** (451), pp. 1–8.

OECD (2013) 'Household debt', in *OECD Factbook 2013: Economic, Environmental and Social Statistics,* Paris: OECD.

OECD (2017a) 'Household debt (indicator)'. doi: 10.1787/f03b6469-en (Accessed: 20 December 2017).

OECD (2017b) 'Wealth statistics'. OECD.Stat. https://stats.oecd.org/Index.aspx?DataSetCode=WEALTH# (Accessed 20 December 2017).

Oksanen, A., Aaltonen, M. and Rantala, K. (2015) 'Social determinants of debt problems in a Nordic welfare state: A Finnish register-based study', *Journal of Consumer Policy,* **38** (3), pp. 229–246.

Patel, A., Balmer, N. J. and Pleasence, P. (2012) 'Debt and disadvantage: The experience of unmanageable debt and financial difficulty in England and Wales', *International Journal of Consumer Studies,* **36**, pp. 556–565.

Piketty, T. (2014) *Capital in the Twenty-First Century.* Cambridge, MA: Belknap Press of Harvard University Press.

Pleasence, P., Balmer, N. J., Buck, A. and Patel, A. (2007) 'Mounting problems: Further evidence of the social, economic and health consequences of civil justice problems', in Pleasence, P., Buck, A. and Balmer, N. J. (eds) *Transforming Lives: Law and Social Process.* Norwich: The Stationery Office.

Polanyi, K. (1944) *The Great Transformation.* New York: Farrar and Rinehart.

Poppe, C. (2008) *Into the Debt Quagmire: How Defaulters Cope with Severe Debt Problems.* Oslo: University of Oslo.

Poppe, C., Lavik, R. and Borgeraas, E. (2016) 'The dangers of borrowing in the age of financialization', *Acta Sociologica,* **56** (1), pp. 19–33.

Poppe, C. and Tufte, P.A. (2005) *Gjeldsordninger i velstands-Norge: En undersøkelse av åpnede gjeldsordningssaker ved Oslo byfogdembete i 1999 og 2004.* SIFO oppdragsrapport nr. 7.

Porter, K. and Thorne, D. (2006) 'The failure of bankruptcy's fresh start', *Cornell Law Review,* **92**, pp. 67–128.

Prasad, M. (2012) *The Land of Too Much: American Abundance and the Paradox of Poverty.* Cambridge, MA: Harvard University Press.

Quinterno, J. (2012) *The Great Cost Shift: How Higher Education Cuts Undermine the Future Middle Class.* New York: Demos.

Raijas, A., Lehtinen, A.-R. and Leskinen, J. (2010) 'Over-indebtedness in Finnish consumer society', *Journal of Consumer Policy,* **33** (3), pp. 209–223.

Ramsay, I. (2017) *Personal Insolvency in the 21st Century: A Comparative Analysis of the US and Europe.* Oxford: Far Publishing.

Rantala, K. and Tarkkala, H. (2009) *Kotitalouksien velkaongelmien nykytila ja kehitys.* Oikeuspoliittisen tutkimuslaitoksen tutkimustiedonantoja 90. Helsinki: Oikeuspoliittinen tutkimuslaitos.

Ratcliffe, C., McKernan, S.-M., Theodos, B., Kalish, E., Chalekian, J., Guo, P. and Trepel, C. (2014) 'Delinquent debt in America'. Urban

Institute. An Opportunity and Ownership Initiative Brief. Urban Institute, 30 July.

Reifner, U. (2000) *Inclusive Contract Law: A Common Law/ Civil Law Joint Venture to Confront Poverty.* Hamburg/New York: IFF.

Reifner, U. (2003) '"Thou shalt pay thy debts": Personal bankruptcy law and inclusive contract law' in Niemi-Kiesiläinen, J., Ramsay, I. and Whitford, W. (eds) *Consumer Bankruptcy in Global Perspective.* Oxford: Hart.

Reiter, M. (2017) *How Creditors Enforce Judgments.* Available at: www.nolo.com/legal-encyclopedia/how-creditors-enforce-judgments. html (Accessed: 27 October 2017).

Richardson, T., Elliott, P. and Roberts, R. (2013) 'The relationship between personal unsecured debt and mental and physical health: A systematic review and meta-analysis', *Clinical Psychology Review,* **33** (8), pp. 1148–1162.

Rogers, J. et al. (2015) 'President's Advisory Council on Financial Capability for Young Americans'. Available at: www.treasury.gov/ resource-center/financial-education/Documents/PACFCYA%20Final% 20Report%20June%202015.pdf.

Rowntree, S. (1901) *Poverty: A Study of Town Life.* London: Macmillan.

Rueger, H., Weishaar, H., Ochsmann, E., Letzel, S. and Muenster, E. (2013) 'Factors associated with self-assessed increase in tobacco consumption among over-indebted individuals in Germany: A cross-sectional study', *Substance Abuse Treatment, Prevention, and Policy,* **8** (12). doi: 10.1186/1747-597X-8-12.

Schwartz, H. (2012) 'Housing, the welfare state, and the global financial crisis: What is the connection?', *Politics & Society,* **40** (1), pp. 35–58.

Selenko, E. and Batinic, B. (2011) 'Beyond debt: A moderator analysis of the relationship between perceived financial strain and mental health', *Social Science and Medicine,* **73** (12), pp. 1725–1732.

Sen, A. (1992) *Inequality Reexamined.* Oxford: Oxford University Press.

Skinner, C., Meyer, D., Cook, K. and Fletcher, M. (2017) 'Child maintenance and social security interactions: The poverty reduction effects in model lone parent families across four countries', *Journal of Social Policy,* **46** (3), pp. 495–516.

Smelser, N. J. and Swedberg, R. (eds) (2005) *The Handbook of Economic Sociology.* Princeton: Princeton University Press.

SNA (2008) *System of National Accounts.* United Nations. Available at: https://unstats.un.org/unsd/nationalaccount/docs/SNA2008.pdf.

Soederberg, S. (2014) *Debtfare States, and the Poverty Industry: Money, Discipline and the Surplus Population.* Abingdon: Routledge.

SOU (2014) *F-skuldsanering – en möjlighet till nystart för seriösa företagare: Statens Offentliga Utredningar SOU 2014:44.* National

Public Inquiry on "An Opportunity for a Fresh Start for Serious Entrepreneurs".

Statistisches Bundesamt (2017) *Statistik zur Überschuldung privater Personen 2016*. Statistisches Bundesamt, Destatis.

Storm, S. and Naastepad, C. (2014) 'Crisis and recovery in the German economy: The real lessons', *Structural Change and Economic Dynamics*, **32**, pp. 11–24.

Stringhini, S., Carmelli, C. Jokela, M ... and Kivimäki, M. (2017) 'Socioeconomic status and the 25 × 25 risk factors as determinants of premature mortality: A multicohort study and meta-analysis of 1·7 million men and women', *Lancet*, **389** (10075), pp. 1229–1237.

Sullivan, T., Warren, E. and Westbrook, J. L. (2000) *The Fragile Middle Class: Americans in Debt*. New Haven: Yale University Press.

Suomen Asiakastieto (2017) *Persons with Payment Defaults 30.6.2017*.

Sweet, E., Nandi, A., Adam, E. and McDaded, T. (2013) 'The high price of debt: Household financial debt and its impact on mental and physical health', *Social Science and Medicine*, **91**, pp. 94–100.

Tanskanen, J. (2015) 'Parental long term over-indebtedness as a predictor for children's psychiatric morbidity: A 13 year follow-up of the 1987 birth cohort'. Master's thesis. University of Helsinki. Available at: https://helda.helsinki.fi/bitstream/handle/10138/155266/Tanskanen_Sosiologia.pdf?sequence=2 (Accessed: 16 November 2017).

Townsend, P. (1979) *Poverty in the United Kingdom*. London: Allen Lane/Penguin.

Trumbull, G. (2012) 'Credit access and social welfare: The rise of consumer lending in the United States and France', *Politics & Society*, **40** (1), pp. 9–34.

Turunen, E. and Hiilamo, H. (2014) Health effects of indebtedness: A systematic review. *BMC Public Health*, **14**, pp. 489ff.

Valkama, E. and Muttilainen, V. (2008) 'Payment difficulties associated with SMS loans'. National Research Institute of Legal Policy, *Research Communications*, **86**, pp. 79–84.

van der Cruijsen, C., de Haan, J. and Jansen, D.-J. (2016) 'Trust and financial crisis experiences', *Social Indicators Research*, **127** (2), pp. 577-600. doi: 10.1007/s11205-015-0984-8.

van Oorschot, W. (2000) 'Who should get what, and why? On deservingness criteria and the conditionality of solidarity among the public', *Policy & Politics*, **28** (1), pp. 33–48.

van Oorschot, W. and Halman, L. (2000) 'Blame or fate, individual or social? An international comparison of popular explanations of poverty', *European Societies*, **2** (1), pp. 1–28.

Vinokur, A. D., Price, R. H. and Caplan, R. D. (1996) 'Hard times and hurtful partners: How financial strain affects depression and relationship satisfaction of unemployed persons and their spouses', *Journal of Personality and Social Psychology,* **71** (1), p. 166–179.

Webley, P. and Nyhus, E. K. (2001) 'Life cycle and dispositional routes into problem debt', *British Journal of Psychology,* **92** (3), pp. 423–446.

Weyerer, S. and Wiedenmann, A. (1995) 'Economic factors and the rates of suicide in Germany between 1881 and 1989', *Psychological Reports,* **76** (3), pp. 1331–1341.

White, J. M. and Klein, D. M. (2002) *Family Theories: Understanding Families* (2nd edn). Thousand Oaks, CA: Sage.

Wilhelmsson, T. (1990*)* 'Social force majeure: A new concept in Nordic consumer law', *Journal of Consumer Policy,* **13** (1), pp. 1–14.

Williams J. (2006) 'Debt education: Bad for the young, bad for America', *Dissent,* **53** (3), pp. 53–59.

Wong, P. W., Chan, W. S., Conwell, Y., Conner, K. R. and Yip, P. S. (2010) 'A psychological autopsy study of pathological gamblers who died by suicide', *Journal of Affective Disorders,* **120** (1–3), pp. 213–216. doi: 10.1016/j.jad.2009.04.001.

World Bank (2013a) *Report on the Treatment of the Insolvency of Natural Persons.* Washington, DC: World Bank.

World Bank (2013b) *Responsible Lending: Overview of Regulatory Tools.* Washington, DC: World Bank. Available at: http://documents. worldbank.org/curated/en/596151468336064796/Responsible-lending-overview-of-regulatory-tools.

Worthington A. C. (2006) 'Debt as a source of financial stress in Australian households', *International Journal of Consumer Studies,* **30** (1), pp. 2–15.

Zinman, J. (2015) 'Household debt: Facts, puzzles, theories, and policies', *Annual Review of Economics,* **7**, pp. 251–276.

Index